OPTIONS TRADING

The Ultimate Guide to Make Money Online Investing in Stock Market. Discover the Benefits of Technical Analysis, Financial Leverage and Risk Management to Generate Passive Income

Andrew Bennett

publisher for any reparation, damages, or monetary loss due to the information herein, either directly or indirectly.

Respective authors own all copyrights not held by the publisher.

The information herein is offered for informational purposes solely and is universal as so. The presentation of the information is without contract or any type of guarantee assurance.

The trademarks that are used are without any consent, and the publication of the trademark is without permission or backing by the trademark owner. All trademarks and brands within this book are for clarifying purposes only and are the owned by the owners themselves, not affiliated with this document.

Table of Contents

Introduction

Stock options and futures are the frequently discussed investment products that people are accustomed to reading about on the market news. In the morning, several professional buyers and traders wake up and look at stock futures to get a feel when the market begins compared to the end of the previous day. In order to see whether profits can be gained by hedging their bets during the trading day, some can look at the price of oil contracts or other commodities.

You might presume that these futures contracts or options markets are another advanced financial tool developed for their disingenuous intentions by Wall Street gurus, but if you did, you would be wrong. In reality, contracts for options and futures did not exist at all on Wall Street. These devices date back hundreds of years to their origins-well before they formally started selling in 1973.

The advent of Futures for Commodity

A futures contract requires the investor to acquire or exchange a given amount of a product at a specified price within a specified time period. Energy, grain, natural gas, wheat, copper, potash, and several other highly traded properties are commodities. These products are extensively used by a large spectrum of market players, starting from Wall Street investors to cultivators who want their agricultural products to generate stable money.

The development of the first completely functioning commodity exchange in the late seventeenth century is attributed to the Japanese. The samurai were paid in rice, not money, for their contributions during this time span. Naturally, they decided to regulate the rice markets, where the rice exchange and trading took place. The samurai had the option to generate a profit on a more stable basis by setting up a regulated market in which sellers and buyers could 'barter' for rice. The samurai began the "Dojima Rice Trade" in 1697, working with other rice brokers. That scheme was quite dissimilar to the Kansai Derivative Trade, the new Japanese agricultural trade.

This book, besides delving into the functions of the Options market, shall touch upon important information with regard to options trading. However, the most important and interesting feature of this book is that, as you read through, it will discuss and describe in detail various trading strategies that will help you to extend your earning potential through the employment of anxiety-free smart options trading techniques.

CHAPTER 1: History of Options Trading

Modern option contracts are generally related to equities. What is a stock option, then, and where did it come from? Simply put, over a defined time frame, a stock option contract grants the holder the right to buy or sell a defined number of shares for a pre-determined price.

In comparison to other traditional types, like buying shares, many people think of trading of options as a relatively new form of investment. As we know, modern options contracts were only really instituted when the Chicago Board of Options Exchange (CBOE) was established, but it is believed that the fundamental concept of options deals was built in Ancient Greece: maybe as long ago as in the mid-4th century BC.

Since then, options have been present in different markets in one way or another, right up until the creation of the CBOE around 1973, when they were appropriately standardized for the earliest time, and trading of options gained some authority. Given below are the details of the history of trading options and options, beginning with Ancient Greece and moving right through to the present day.

Thales and the Olive Harvest

A book printed in the mid-4th century by Aristotle, a Greek

philosopher of huge influence and author of many subjects, provides the earliest recorded example of options trading. Aristotle consists of an account of another theorist, Thales of Miletus, and how he earned from an olive harvest in this book, entitled "Politics."

Thales had a great interest in mathematics and astronomy, among other things, and he merged his knowledge of those subjects to make what were the earliest known option contracts effectively. Thales predicted by studying the stars that there would be a massive olive harvest in his area and set out to benefit from his prediction. He acknowledged that there would be a major need for olive presses and intended to corner the market fundamentally.

Thales, however, did not have sufficient funds to own all the olive presses, so instead, he paid each olive press owner a sum of money to get the rights to make use of them at the time of harvest. Thales's rights were resold to olive presses by him to persons who required them and made a considerable profit when harvest time came around, and as Thales had forecast, it was indeed a huge harvest.

Though the term was not applied at the time, with olive presses as the underlying security, Thales had successfully made the first call option. He had paid for the right to make use of the olive presses at a fixed price, but not the obligation, and was then able to practice his options for revenue. This is the fundamental principle of how requests work today; we now have other variables, such as financial instruments and commodities, as the core security instead of olive presses.

Tulip Bulb Mania in the 17th Century

Another related event in the past of options was an incident in Holland in the 17th century that is commonly referred to as Tulip Bulb Mania. Tulips were very popular in that region at the time and were thought of as symbols of status among the Dutch gentry. Their fame had also spread to Europe and around the world, and this had headed to a dramatic increase in the need for tulip bulbs.

By this point in the past, calls and puts, mainly for hedging purposes, were used in various markets. Tulip growers, for example, would purchase puts to safeguard their revenues just in case the cost of tulip bulbs went down. The tulip wholesalers would then purchase calls to guard against the risk of rising tulip bulb prices. It should be noted that these agreements were not as advanced as they are today, and the markets for options were comparatively informal and entirely unregulated.

The need for tulip bulbs remained to increase during the 1630s, and the price also increased in value because of this. As a result, the cost of tulip bulb options' bonds rose, and a secondary market arose for these deals that allowed anyone to wonder on the tulip bulb market. In Holland, many people and families invested heavily in these contracts, frequently using all their money or even borrowing from resources like their property.

The cost of tulip bulbs continued to increase, but not for so long could it continue, and the bubble eventually burst. Prices had gone up to the end where they were unsustainable, and as prices began to fall, buyers began to disappear. So many of those who had put the cost of tulip bulbs at risk were totally wiped out. They lost all their wealth and their dwellings to ordinary people. The economy of the Netherlands also entered a recession.

There was no other way to push investors to meet their option contract's obligations because the options market was unregulated, and this eventually led to options earning a poor reputation worldwide.

Bans on Options Trading

Options still held an appeal for many investors, regardless of the bad name that these contracts had. This was mainly because they were provided excellent leverage power, that is truly one of the grounds why today they are so common. So, the trading of these contracts resumed to take place, but their bad repute could not be dispelled. Increased disapproval of their use was also expressed.

In many parts of the world, options have been prohibited several times throughout history: mainly in Japan, Europe, and even in certain states in America. The most remarkable of the bans, perhaps, was in London, England. Opposition to them was not overcome in the late 1600s, despite the emergence of an integrated sector for calls and placements, and options were eventually made unlawful in the early 18th century.

This prohibition lasted more than a hundred years and was not raised until later in the 19th century.

Jesse Livermore's investing philosophy

The bucket shop in America in the 1920s was made famous by a man named Jesse Livermore. Options seem to have made their debut in the USA through what was described as "bucket shops." Livermore speculated on the movements in stock prices; he did not own the securities on which he was betting but merely forecast their future prices. He was a stock option bookie at the beginning of his career, taking the opposite side of anyone who thought a specific stock might rise or decrease in price. If someone came to him speculating that the stock of

XYZ Company was going to go up, he would opt for the reverse side.

The investing philosophy of Jesse Livermore was not foolproof, but he is still recognized as one of the greatest traders in history.

Russell Sage and Put & Call Brokers

A significant change in the account of options trading is associated with an American financier by the name of Russell Sage. In the late 19th century, Sage started making calls and options that might be traded in the US over the counter. There was no formal exchange market yet, but Sage generated action that was a breakthrough for the trading of options.

It is also thought that Sage is the leading person to set up a pricing relation between an option's price, the underlying security's price, and interest rates. To develop synthetic loans that were made by him through the purchasing of securities and an associated put from a client, he used the principle of put-call parity.

This made it possible for him to loan money effectively to the client at an interest amount that he could decide by fixing the contract price and the appropriate strike prices consequently. Due to significant losses, Sage ultimately ceased trading in his path, but he was instrumental in the continual evolution of the trading of options.

Dealers and Brokers began to place advertisements during the late 1800s to attract sellers and buyers of options contracts with a viewpoint to brokering contracts. The concept was that the broker would be contacted by a concerned party and show their concern in buying either puts or calls on a specific stock. On the other side of the transaction, the broker would then seek to find someone.

This was somehow a laborious procedure, and the two related parties essentially determined the terms of each contract. In order to establish systems that could help in matching sellers and buyers of contracts more efficiently, the Put and Call Brokers and Dealers Association was formed, but still, there was no baseline for rating them, and there was a noticeable lack of market liquidity.

By this point, the options trading was surely growing, although the dearth of any rule meant that shareholders were still cautious.

The Listed Options Market

Put and call brokers continued to essentially control the market for options, with deals being traded over the stall. In the market, there was some consistency, and more individuals got conscious of these agreements and their possible uses. With restricted action at this time, the market remained relatively illiquid.

The brokers made their revenues from the spread between whatever the buyers were prepared to give and what the brokers were prepared to accept, but there was no specific right price system, and it was easy for the brokers to set the spread as large as they liked.

While the Securities and Exchange Commission (SEC) in the US had introduced some regulations in the market for over the security options, by the early 1960s, their trading was not really advancing at any visible rate. Too many complications were involved, and unpredictable values had also made it very hard for any stockholder to take options seriously as a feasible tradable tool.

In 1968, it was an essentially unrelated event that eventually led to a solution that would eventually bring the market for options into the mainstream.

The Chicago Board of Trade experienced a major decline in commodity futures trading on its exchange in 1968, and the organization started to look for innovative ways to excel in its business. The objective was to expand and create further trade opportunities for exchange members. The decision was taken, after considering a few alternatives, to establish a formal exchange for the exchange of options contracts.

For this to become possible, there were several barriers to overcome, but the Chicago Board of Options Exchange (CBOE) started trading in 1973. Options deals were adequately standardized for the first time, and there was a good market for them to be operated. At the same time, for centralized clearing and ensuring the appropriate completion of contracts, the Options Clearing Corporation was created. Finally, it was more than 2,000 years after the first call was made by Thales. That finally led to the legitimacy of options trading.

Evolution of Options Trading

There were very few contracts listed when the CBOE opened for trading, and they were just calling because, at this point, puts were not standardized. The idea of trading options was also still somewhat opposed, largely due to problems in verifying whether they presented a good amount for money.

The absence of a clear method for analyzing a fair option price, blended with widespread, required that there was still a lack of liquidity in the market. Another important growth helped to alter that in a little time after the opening of the CBOE for trading.

Two professors, Myron Scholes and Fisher Black designed a mathematical formula in that same year of 1973. The formula was good enough to compute the Options price by using standardized variables. As investors began to feel more comfortable trading options, this formulation became known as the Black Scholes Pricing Model, and it had a great impact.

The daily volume of agreements traded on the CBOE was above 20,000 by 1974, and two more trading floors of options were opened in America in 1975. The sum of stocks on which options could be exchanged was risen in 1977, and puts on the exchanges were also launched. More option trades were formed around the globe in the following years, and the variety of contracts that could be exchanged continued to develop.

Online trading began to gain popularity near the end of the 20th century, which made the trading of various financial tools far more accessible to participants of the public across the world. With a huge number of professional and amateur traders, the quality and quantity of the electronic brokers accessible on the web expanded, and electronic options trading became famous.

There are hundreds of contracts that are being listed on the trades in the modern options market, and millions of contracts trade every day. Trading in options continues to increase in fame and reveals no signs of reducing.

The regulatory framework for Options

In the beginning, rampant illegal activities plagued the commodity futures markets and stock options markets. Today, the most traded options are on the Chicago Board of Options Exchange (CBOE). Like stock markets, the activities of options markets draw a great deal of scrutiny from regulatory agencies such as the SEC and, in some cases, from the FBI. The market for commodities today is also tightly controlled. The Commodity Exchange Act prohibits the illegal trading of futures contracts and, through the Commodity Futures Trading Commission, mandates the particular procedures required in the industry. A variety of problems concern regulatory agencies, many of which stem from the highly computerized nature of today's trading environment. In order to create an "even" playing field for all investors, price-fixing and collusion are still problems that the agencies try to prohibit.

Bottom line

In scope and sophistication, today's futures markets vary greatly from the barter schemes that were first set up by the Japanese. Advances in technology have produced trading options and futures readily available to the average investor, as you might suspect. Most options and futures are electronically executed and go through the Options Clearing Corporation

(OCC), a clearing agency. Their global reach is another aspect of today's options and futures markets. Most big states have futures markets and exchanges of futures on products ranging from weather, commodities, stocks, and now even returns from Hollywood films. The futures market has global breadth, the same as the stock market. It is not without consequence to globalize futures exchanges. Fundamentals and psychology of the market went down with incredible intensity, as we saw during the meltdowns of the last decade, mainly due to product securities. The results for the stock and futures markets might have been too worse had there been no government intervention.

CHAPTER 2: Learn about Options and Basics of Options Trading

Options are securities that grant the investor the option to purchase or sell an asset at a predetermined price, called the strike price, over a specified period of time, without any specific precondition. The amount of time may be as brief as a day, or as lengthy as a few years, depending on the form of contract available. There are only two forms of regular contracts with options: a call and a put.

Trading options is simple to understand, as long as you learn certain important points. Investor portfolios are generally built with multiple asset classes. These could include stocks, bonds, ETFs and even mutual funds. Options are another asset class and offer many advantages that trading stocks and ETFs alone cannot possibly offer when used correctly.

2.1 Salient Features of Options

Like other asset classes, options can be purchased with an investment account. Options are strong because they can improve the portfolio of an individual. They do this by adding income, providing safeguards and even leverage. Depending, there is typically a scenario of options tailored to the target of an investor. To limit downside losses, a common example would be to use options as an efficient hedge against a decreasing stock market. Also, options can be used to produce recurring profits. In addition, they are commonly used for gambling reasons, such as wagering on stock direction. Trading of options involves certain risks that the investor must be aware of before making a trade. Options involve risks and are not appropriate for everyone. Trading of options may be risky in nature and bear a significant risk of failure.

• An option is a contract that gives the buyer the right, but not the obligation, to buy or sell (in the case of a call) the underlying asset at a specific price on or before a specific date.

• Traders use income, speculation and risk-hedging options.

• Options are also referred to as derivatives since they derive their value from the underlying assets.

• A stock option contract usually comprises 100 percent of the underlying stock, but options can be drawn upon some type of underlying properties, from debt to currency to product.

Customization is all about trading with options. Rewards may be big, but so can the danger, so there's plenty to choose from. But it's not easy to get started, and there is potential for pricey errors.

2.2 Types of Options

There are two options. It is important to note; the owner is not obliged to exercise his or her right to buy or sell for both types of options contracts. A brief description and roles of each are given below:

Call Option

A call option contract grants the owner the right to purchase 100 shares of specified security within a specified time frame at a specified price. A call option provides you the right to buy a stock at a certain price by a specific date, with the expiration option. The call buyer will give a sum of cash called a premium for this right, which the call supplier will get. Not Like stocks that can live in perpetuity, after expiration, an option will stop to exist, ending either worthlessly or with some worth.

Components of Call Option

The following elements contain the major characteristics of an option:

Strike price

At this price, you will purchase the underlying stock

Premium

The cost of the option, for the buyer or the seller

Expiration

It is when the option runs out and is settle down

How does a Call Option Work

Each option is considered a deal, and the underlying stock contains 100 securities in each deal. Exchanges quote options in terms of interest per unit, not the overall amount you have to pay to buy the deal. For example, on the exchange, an option might be estimated at $0.75. And it would cost (100 shares * 1 contract * $0.75), or $75 to purchase one contract.

If the purchase price is over the strike price at maturity, the call options are in the bank. The call owner may practice the option, putting up cash at the strike price to buy the stock. Or the possessor can actually sell the right to another buyer at its reasonable market price.

A call owner gains on less than the distinction between the strike price and the stock price when the premium is paid. Suppose, for starters, that a dealer purchased a $0.50 call with a $20 strike price, and that supply is $23. The option valued at $3 and the trader made revenue of 2.50 dollars.

If the purchase price at maturity falls below the selling amount, otherwise the call is out of the market and expires. The call seller retains the option for any premium obtained.

Put Option

A put option contract gives the owner the right to sell within a given time frame 100 shares of a specified security at a specified price. Each contract represents 100 shares or the stock on which the option is based. Putting options enables traders to magnify downward market changes, transforming a slight price decline into a big benefit for the put buyer.

Components of Put Option

The following components contain the major characteristics of an option:

Strike price

The price at which you will sell the underlying stock

Premium

The cost of the option, for either the buyer or the seller

Expiration

When the option runs out and is settled

How does a Put Option Work

For that privilege, the put buyer pays the put seller a premium per share. At expiry, if the price of the stock is lower than the price of the strike, the put value grows in money. The interest of the put, in this case, is proportional to the strike price minus the selling price times 100, as each contract contains 100 securities. Unless the price of the stock is greater than the strike, the put is useless.

Options as Derivatives

The options belong to the broader financial community, known as derivatives. The price of a derivative depends on or is derived from the price of something else. A stock choice is equity derivative. Options are financial securities derivatives-their value depends on some other asset's price

Buying and Selling Calls/Puts

There are four things you could do with options:

- Purchase Calls

- Sell calls

- Buy puts

- Sell puts

Buying stock provides a long position for you. Buying a call option will give you a potentially long position in the underlying stock. Short selling of stock provides you with a short position. Selling a naked or uncovered call in the underlying stock gives you a potential short position.

Buying a put option in the underlying stock gives you a

potentially short position. Selling a put option gives you a theoretically long place in the stock underlying it.

Those who purchase options are classified as investors, and others who offer options are named options writers. Here's the big difference between holders and writers:

There is no requirement for call investors and put investors (buyers) to buy or sell. They are granted the opportunity to exercise their privileges. This reduces the chance of options owners to just paying the premium.

However, call writers and put writers (sellers) are obliged to buy or sell if the option expires. This means a seller may need to make good on a purchase or sell pledge. It also means that sellers of options are subject to additional and, in certain situations, infinite threats. It ensures writers will risk a lot more than the quality of premium options.

Options Expiration & Liquidity

Also, options can be categorized according to their duration. Short-term options are options which usually terminate within one year. Long-term options with expirations longer than one year are known as shares where the holder hopes for a jump in price in the long-term. LEAPS are similar to standard solutions; they simply last longer.

Also, options can be distinguished when their expiry date falls. Sets of options also regularly expire on a Monday, at month's end, or even hourly. Index and ETF choices also often sell expiries annually.

American and European Options

American options can be exercised at any period between the acquisition date and the expiry date. European alternatives vary from American choices in that they should only be used on the termination day at the close of their expiry time. The difference between American and European options has nothing to do with geography. Many equity indexing options are European-style. Since the right to exercise early has some value, an American option typically carries a premium higher than a European option, which is otherwise identical. This is because the feature of early exercise is desirable and commands a premium.

Speculation

A speculator might think a stock's price will rise on the basis of fundamental analysis or technical analysis. A speculator may purchase stock or purchase a call on the stock option. Speculating with an incentive to call — rather than purchasing the stock directly — is appealing to certain traders because options have leverage. An out-of-the-money call option will pay just a few bucks, or just cents, relative to a $100 full stock price.

Hedging

Hedging with options is intended to reduce risk at a reasonable expense. Say you intend to buy inventories of equipment. Yet you do want losses to be minimal. You will reduce the downside exposure by utilizing put options and reap all the upside in a cost-effective manner. Call options may be used by short sellers to reduce losses if incorrect-particularly during a short squeeze.

2.3 Advantages of Options Trading

Options provide more planned (and economic) leeway to investors than they can get by selling, buying or shorting stocks. Traders can use portfolio loss protection options, snag security for less than it manages to sell on the open marketplace (or offer it for more), maximize the total returns on a current or new position, and reduce the risk of speculative betting under all kinds of market situations.

Yes, in the pros vs. cons of options trading, there are a lot of positives. But there are inherent risks as well. Here are some things that should be considered by every prospective options trader.

It requires a lower financial commitment as compared to stock trading

The cost of purchasing an option (the premium along with the trading commission) is much lower than what a trader would have to pay to buy shares directly.

Traders pay less money to play in the same sandbox, but they will gain just as much (percentage - wise) if the trade goes their way as the trader who shelled out for the stock.

There's the limited downside for buyers of options

You are not required to follow through on the trade when you purchase a put or call option. If your assumptions are incorrect about the time frame and direction of the trajectory of stock, your losses are limited to anything you paid for the contract as well as trading fees. For options sellers, however, the downside can be much higher.

Options offer built-in flexibility for traders

Before the expiry of an options contract, investors have the liberty to use various strategic moves, including:

- Use the option and purchase the shares to add to their portfolio

- Use the option, purchase the shares and then sell some or all of them

- Sell the "in the money" options contract to a different investor

- Has the option to recover some of the money incurred on an "out of the money" option. This can be done by selling the contract to another investor before its expiry

Options enable an investor to fix a stock price

Options contracts allow investors to freeze the stock price at a specific amount of dollars (the strike price) for a specific period of time in an action similar to putting something on layaway. Based on the type of option used, it ensures that investors will be able to purchase the stock at the strike price any time before the expiry of the option contract.

2.4 Drawbacks of Options Trading

Given below are some of the disadvantages of options trading that must be taken into consideration, especially by a beginner.

Options expose sellers to extreme losses

Contrary to an option buyer (or holder), -losses of much greater value- than the price of the contract- can be incurred by the option seller (writer). Remember, when an investor opts to write a put or call at a predetermined price, he or she is required to purchase or sell shares within the time frame irrespective of the fact whether the price is in his favor or against.

Options are time-specific

Short term is the basic essence of options. Investors of options are seeking to benefit from a near-term market change that could take place for the trade/contract to generate pay off within days, weeks or months. This requires two correct decisions to be made: determining the best time to obtain the option contract and determining specifically whether to exercise, sell or step away before the offer expires. There isn't a deadline for long-term equity buyers. They have time to let their investment play out for years, even decades.

Pre-requisites for potential traders

You must apply for clearance from your broker before even starting trading options. The broker may grant you a trading class that determines what kinds of options trades you are permitted to place after addressing a number of questions regarding your financial capital, investing background and your knowledge on the inherent risks of trading options. Any trader who is into options' trading must hold in their trading account a minimum of $2,000, which is an industry-standard and a cost of investment worth contemplating.

Options' trading involves additional costs

Any trading strategy for options (such as selling call options on stocks you don't actually own) enables buyers to set up a margin account, which is simply a line of credit that acts as collateral in the event that the transaction shifts against the investor. For the opening of a margin account, each brokerage company has various minimum conditions and may base the sum and interest rate on how much cash and shares are in the account. Usually, margin loan interest rates may range between the low single digits and the low double digits.

If an investor is unwilling to make good on loan (or if the value of the trading account falls below a certain amount, which may happen due to regular market fluctuations), if he or she does not add more cash or securities to it, the lender may trigger a margin call and liquidate an investor's portfolio.

The Options Clearing Corporation offers a comprehensive overview of the features and risks of standardized options and an overview of the U.S. federal income tax rules that impact those looking to invest in options and other financial products.

Bottom line

You must recognize the company's market inside out and determine whether to purchase, sell or retain stock for the long term and have a good understanding of the way the asset is going. Investors of options ought to be hyper-aware of those items and more.

Success in options demands from investors to have a clear idea of the inherent value of the firm, but perhaps most significantly, they will need to have a sound thesis of how the business has been and would be impacted by short-term variables such as internal activities, sector/competition, and macroeconomic impacts.

Many investors can conclude that options offer their financial lives with excessive uncertainty. But the options trading strategies for beginners can help limit your downside if you are interested in exploring the possibilities that options offer and have the right discipline and the capital to endure potential losses.

2.5 Basics of Options' Pricing

The value of stock options is determined from their underlying shares' value and, depending on the results of the associated shares, the trading price for options can increase or decrease. With options, there are a variety of elements to understand.

The Strike Price

The strike price for an option is the rate at which, if the option is exercised, the underlying asset is purchased or sold. In the peculiar jargon of options, the relationship between the strike price and a stock's market price determines the following:

- Option is in-the-money

- Options are at-the-money

- Option is out-of-the-money

In-the-money

The strike price of an in-the-money call option is below the real market price. Example: At the $95 strike price for WXYZ, an investor buys a call option that is already trading at $100. The investor's position is $5 in-the-money. The call option grants the investor the right to purchase the shares at $95. The strike price of an In-the-Money Put option is above the real market price. Example: At the WXYZ's $110 strike price, which is currently trading at $100, an investor buys a Put option. In-the-money is $10 for this investor position. The Put option grants the seller the right to sell equity at $110.

At the money

For both Put and Call options, the strike and the actual stock prices are the same.

Out-of-the-money

The strike price of an out-of-the-money call option is above the real market price. Example: At the strike price of $120 for ABCD, which is actually trading at $105, an investor buys an out-of-the-money call option. The position of this investor is $15 out-of-the-money. The strike price of an out-of-the-money put option is below the real market price. Example: At the $90 strike price of ABCD, which is currently priced at $105, an investor buys an out-of-the-money Put option. The position of that investor is $15 out-of-the-money.

The Premium

The premium is the price for an option that a customer pays to the seller. On purchasing, the premium is paid upfront and is not reimbursable-even though the option is not applied. Premiums on a per-share base are quoted. So, a $0.21 premium reflects a $21.00 per option contract ($0.21 x 100 shares) premium payment. There are many considerations that decide the amount of the premium-the prevailing stock price in comparison to the strike price (intrinsic value), the period of time before the offer expires (time value) and the price fluctuations of the commodity (volatility value).

Intrinsic value + Value of time + Value of volatility = option price

For example, at a strike price of $80, an investor buys a three-month call option for volatile security that trades at $90.

Intrinsic Value = $10

Time value = because the call is 90 days away, the time value will be slightly applied to the price.

Volatility value = Because the underlying security is volatile, the volatility premium might be added.

Factors that influence options prices

The following factors have an impact on options prices:

- The underlying equity price in relation to the strike price (intrinsic value)

- The length of time until the option expires (time value)

- How much the price fluctuates (volatility value)

Ancillary factors that influence option prices

- Additional facts that have an impact on options prices are:

- The underlying equity's quality

- The underlying equity's dividend rate

- Prevailing market conditions

- The underlying equity's supply and demand for options

- The existing interest rates

Additional costs: Taxes and commissions

Investors that trade options, as in virtually any investment, must pay income taxes and also commissions to brokers on options trades. The net profit gain would be impacted by these costs.

2.6 Pricing Spreads in Options and Trading Strategies

A call spread relates to the purchasing of a call on a strike, and the selling of another call for a higher strike of the same expiry. An option strategy in which a call option is purchased is a call spread, and another less costly call option is sold.

A put spread relates to purchasing a put on strike and selling another put on the same expiry's lower price. An option technique in which a put option is purchased is a put spread, and another less costly put option is sold.

This transaction is less dangerous than an outright buy since the call and put options have identical features, but it often provides less benefit. If you think that the underlying price will shift in a certain direction, and wish to reduce your original outlay if the forecast is wrong, these techniques are beneficial to try.

Advantages of Spreads

When you want to mitigate risk, spreads are useful for trading. Typically, spreads are traded by arbitragers to gain an edge on the transaction with close strikes and then control the position. The position takes in trading premiums as the short option premium tends to cover the cost of the long option.

Call spreads buying considerations

Consider buying call spreads in the following situations:

If you are sure that the underlying security is destined to go up after which volatility will subside (e.g., a news event)

When you are sure that the underlying security is definitely going to edge up moderately

When you are sure that the underlying security's price will decline sharply, thus generating a sale of the underlying security

Consequently, the call spread will guard you against a petty upside move

Put spreads buying considerations

Consider buying put spreads in the following situations:

If you are sure that the underlying security is going to edge downward, resulting in a decrease in volatility (e.g., a news event)

If you are sure that the underlying security is going to depict a decline in a limited range

If you are sure that the underlying security is going to fall sharply

Bull call spread

One long call, along with a lower strike price plus one short call at a higher strike price, is a bull call spread. The very underlying stock and the same expiry period are required for both calls. For a net debit (or net cost) and gains as the underlying stock increases in price, a bull call spread is built. Profit is impaired if the stock price rises above the short call strike price, and the possible loss is restricted if the stock price moves below the long call strike price (lower risk).

Bear Call Spread

A bear call spread, or bear call credit spread, is a form of the strategy of options that are used when an options trader assumes the cost of the main stock to fall. By buying call options at a particular strike price while selling the same amount of calls at the same maturity date, but at a shorter strike price, a bear call spread is established. Using this technique, the utmost

profit to be made is equivalent to the credit earned while starting the trade.

A short call spread is another name for a bear call spread. It is deemed as a strategy with limited-risk and limited-reward.

Calendar call spreads

You sell and purchase a call with the same strike price while running a calendar spread with calls, but the call you purchase would have a later date of expiry than the call you sell. As expiration approaches, you take advantage of accelerating time decay on the front-month call, also known as a shorter-term call. You want to purchase back the shorter-term call right before the front-month expiration for almost nothing. You will sell the back-month call and close your position at the same moment. Ideally, there would also be considerable time value for the back-month call.

Create your calendar spread with at-the-money calls if you're expecting limited price change. Use marginally out-of-the-money calls if you're moderately bullish. This will help you with lower up-front costs.

Bear Put Spread

A bear put spread consists of a higher strike price for one long put and a lower strike price for one short put. Both puts have the same underlying stock and the same expiry date. For a net debit (or net cost) and earnings as the underlying stock decreases in price, a bear put spread is created. Profit is restricted if the stock price falls below the lower strike price of the short put strike), and if the stock price rises above the longput strike price (higher strike), the possible loss is limited.

Bull Put spread

A bull put spread consists of a higher strike price for a short put and a lower strike price for a long put. Both puts have the same underlying security and the same expiry date. For a net credit (or net sum received) and gains from either an increasing equity price or from time erosion or from both, a bull put spread is created. A potential benefit is restricted to the net premium earned fewer commissions, and potential loss is reduced if the stock price drops below the longput strike price.

Calendar put spread

By purchasing one "longer-term" put and selling one "shorter-term" put with the same strike price, a long calendar spread with puts is established. Consider the following example. 100 Put is bought for two months (56 days to expiration), and 100 Put is sold for one month (28 days to expiration). For a net debt (net cost), this strategy is established, and both the profit opportunity and the risk are minimal. If the stock price matches the strike price of the puts on the closing date of the short put, the maximum profit is obtained, and the maximum risk is achieved if the stock price shifts sharply away from the strike price.

2.7 Buying a Call Option

The buyer of an option call search to generate revenue if and when the price of the underlying profit rises to a price higher than the strike price of the option. On the other hand, the call option seller expects the asset's price will fall, or at least never raise as much as the strike/exercise price value until it ends, in which case the money earned for selling the choice would be pure income. If the price of the fundamental safety does not rise above the strike price before expiry, then the option will not be cost-effective for the purchaser to exercise the option, and the option will end valueless or "out of the money." The buyer experiences a loss equivalent to the cost given for the call option. Otherwise, if the cost of the fundamental protection falls past the strike price, the investor may exercise this choice profitably.

For example, imagine you've purchased an option on 100 stocks, with a $30 option to hit before your option runs out; the stock price increases from $28 - $40. You will then exercise the right to purchase 100 stock options at $30, granting you an instant $10 a shared benefit. Your overall income will be 100 options, $10 for a share, minus the sales price you were charged for the option. If you had paid $200 for the call option in this case, then your net income will be $800 (100 shares x $10 per share-$ 200 = $800).

Buying call options helps buyers to spend a small sum of money to theoretically gain from a price increase in the basic safety, or to guard against the positional risks.

Swing traders can use options to transform small quantities of money into large profits, while business and institutional shareholders make use of options to boost their marginal profits.

2.8 Selling a Call Option

Sellers of call options, called writers, offer call options in the expectation that they may become useless by the expiration date. They earn money by pocketing the rates (prices) they have been paying. An income will be lowered, or possibly turn into a net loss if the option holder performs the option profitably as the fundamental safety price falls past the option strike point. The call options are offered in two ways:

Covered Call Option

If the call option seller owns the underlying stock, then a call option is covered. Selling the call options on these fundamental securities brings in extra gain, which would mitigate any anticipated market price decreases. The seller option is "covered" against failure since, in the event that the buyer option exercises its option, the seller can give the buyer with stock shares, which he has already bought at a cost below the option's strike price. The seller's income is holding the underlying stock would be restricted to raising the stock to the strike price, but he will be shielded from any real loss.

Naked Call Option

If a trader of options offers a call option without buying the underlying stock, a naked call option is provided. Naked short-selling options are Known as dangerous when there is no cap on how big a stock's price can go, and the seller of the option is not "covered" by keeping the underlying stock against potential losses. When a call option investor uses his or her privilege, the naked option seller is obliged to acquire the stock at the existing market price to supply the option owner with the securities. If the stock price surpasses the strike price of the call option, then the change between the current market price and the strike price signifies the seller's loss. Most option sellers command a high cost to offset any possible losses.

2.9 Selling and Buying a Put Option

You can produce double-digit income and gains by selling put options even in a smooth, bearish or overrated market. For big returns on investment, you don't need a strong market or speedy business growth. In the case of a market collapse, you may even grant your investments a 10 percent guarantee against the downside. In other words, if the market falls by 25%, your equity locations are likely to fall by only 15%. You can also enter stock positions exactly at the cost you need and keep the cost base low. You should try to purchase in a declining market to get a greater bargain instead of buying at presently available market rates. Like any device, there is a perfect period and place for selling put options, and at certain times, it is not an optimal strategy. This is a sophisticated and best way of entering equity positions when used correctly.

To option sellers, the two most critical things are the strike and the bid. The strike is the amount you agree to buy the shares for if the option is exercised, and the bid is about the amount you can expect to earn on selling the option. If you sell an option with a strike price of $30 below the current stock price of $30.50, you will now receive $143 from the option buyer, and you will be obliged to purchase 100 shares of the company at $30 each if the buyer wishes, for a total of $3,000, at any time before the option expires in 3.5 months.

If the particular company's stock generally stays above $30 / share over the next 3.5 months, the option buyer probably won't assign the shares to you, as there would be no reason for her to force you to pay exactly $30 / share when the market price is already above $30 / share. Her option will expire worthlessly, you will keep your $143 premium, and your $3,000 in secured cash will be released for another option to be sold. Here is the calculated rate of return, if the right expires: $143 / $2,857 = 0.05 = 5%

After around 3.5 months, you made a return yield of 5 percent on your initial currency. This will be around 18 percent annualized returns on your investment if you practice that for the remainder of the year a few times. Compare this with the historical return of the S&P 500 of around 9%. Compared to average stock returns, you're being charged a huge amount of money to only hang around and wait for a market drop on a business you'd like to buy. On the contrary, if the stock dips to $29.50 / share, you still have to retain the $143 premium, and

the buyer option will assign you to purchase the 100 shares for $30 each.

This means that your effective cost base for buying those shares was only $28.57, which, as you wanted, is below your target buy price. You ended up having to purchase them for $30 apiece, but you still got a $1.43 / share bonus upfront, which covered some of the expenses. The total cost structure is that for 100 securities, you have to spend $28.57 / share, or $2.857. So instead, you hold 100 shares of a company already selling for $29.50 each. You purchased a wonderful business at a decent price, and ideally, you should still anticipate lots of growth in profits and dividends over time.

2.10 Collars

A collar option technique, also known as a hedge wrapper or just collar, is an options strategy used to minimize an underlying asset's both positive and negative returns. It restricts the return of the portfolio to a defined range and may hedge the position against the underlying asset's potential volatility. The use of a protective put and covered call option produces a collar position. It is produced more precisely by keeping an underlying stock, purchasing an option that is out of the money, and selling an option that is out of the money call.

The method-Creating a Collar Position

The collar position is created by using the following method:

Collar Position=Long Underlying Asset + Long Put Option + Short Call Option

2.11 Combinations

A combination is a type of an options trading strategy that entails both purchasing and selling of call and put options on the same underlying stock.

Call & Put Buying Combinations

Following are the call and put buying combinations:

Straddle

The straddle is an infinite profit, low-risk options trading technique that is utilized anytime the trader in options expects that the underlying asset price can make a big shift in the price in the immediate future in any direction. By purchasing an equivalent sum of at-the-money call and put options of the same expiration date, it can be established.

Strangle

Strangle is also a technique of limited risk and infinite profit potential, like the straddle. The distinction between the two tactics is that out-of-the-money options are bought to build the strangle, minimizing the cost of maintaining the position, while at the same time needing a significantly greater change in the price of the underlying to be lucrative for the strategy.

CHAPTER 3: Getting ready to Start Options Trading

If you're thinking about trading options for generating profits, you may wonder if it's a decent time to start trading. Guidelines are available that you could always follow.

Get out of Debt

Get out of debt first. Pay off the car loans and credit card balances, explicitly. It's because of those loans; you're losing income anyway.

Instances of' good debt' are known to be leases and student loans, while auto loans and credit card balances are perceived as instances of' bad debt.'

The bottom line is that, before you start trading options, you must get out of bad debt.

Don't Learn the Hard Way

You're also not fully in a spot to trade options even after you've eliminated the bad debt. You first have to know yourself. And if you believe you're ready and in the past you traded stocks; you still aren't done.

Trading options are totally separate from trading securities. And before you trade options, you have to understand the stock market; however, you still need to learn quite a bit more. Start by studying the essentials. Understand the distinction between options for calls and options for put. Know about expiration dates for contracts and strike prices.

The trading of options is for persons who delve extensively into the data to assess the most advantageous trades. Traders who overlook certain stats are sometimes burnt. When you've mastered the basics, it's time to learn about various options strategies.

- Spreads

- Straddles

- Strangles

- Iron butterflies

- Iron condors

- Never Stop Learning

When it applies to options trading, you have never "arrived." There is always something that an expert trader will learn from you. Keep practicing also though you have trained yourself and mastered trading to the extent that you value your expertise as a trader. Strive to make yourself a greater trader every day.

Practice Makes Perfect

Before you allocate real capital, you need to do some practice trading. This is because, before doing the real thing, everybody wants to do some practice trading.

When you invest in the capital markets, there are things you can learn. The quick way rather than the rough way is easier to learn such lessons.

Fortunately, trading platforms are accessible that enable you to learn to trade. Without losing some of your hard-earned assets, you can establish a pretend portfolio and begin trading stocks and options. And, as time progresses, you will see how the trades are successful. Take the time to assess what went wrong if you're not profitable so that you can stop making such errors in the future.

3.1 Educate yourself on requirements for opening an Options trading account

Stock market options are limited-term contracts that offer owners the right to purchase or sell particular securities at a fixed date. In a broad variety of market techniques, the two forms of options — puts and calls — may be used to benefit from potential shifts in equity prices. To start purchasing and selling puts and calls, you must first register for account authorization.

A trading account for options is a cash, margin or IRA stock brokerage account to which trading authorization for options has been applied. By completing a separate document, you incorporate options permission, plus a declaration of your trading background. The regulatory department of the broker checks the application for options and accepts your account with a degree of trading permission varying from one to five. What options strategies may be traded in the account are decided by the authorization levels. Novice investors can obtain one or two levels of authorization that enable strategies for lower-risk options.

3.2 Learn on how to read and execute options contracts

Option contracts are purchased and sold using the online investment account's options trading screen. Under the options-chain link of a given stock, various put and call option choices can be identified. Choosing an option from the chain fills the trading screen with the specifics of a single option. You may then decide how many contracts you choose to purchase or sell and, if necessary, set a cap price. For a market order, the currently quoted "bid" price of an option is what you will pay to purchase. If you sell on the market, the "bid" price is what you would get. Each option contract is on an underlying stock of 100 securities, so one contract costs 100 times the quoted amount.

3.3 Get informed on open and close orders

To start a trading position, options may be either bought or sold. Buying options grants you the right to purchase (call options) and/or sell (put options) the actual stock securities at a particular amount. If the customer uses his privileges under the options you have sold, trading options add option premium earnings to the portfolio and the obligation to sell or purchase stock. You execute a buy-to-open or sell-to-open order to open an options position, depending on your approach. The order would be a sell-to-close or buy-to-close to close an options position in your portfolio.

3.4 Look for the minimum amount required to trade options

To trade options, each online broker needs a different minimum balance. The mandatory minimum deposit for most brokerages is less than $1,000. Investors fill out a brief questionnaire inside their investment account to submit for options trading authorization. It is possible to get access to begin executing options directly afterward.

Options Trading Platforms

To an online broker, there is no consumer more important than an options investor. Trades of options give brokers far larger operating profits than equity trades, and competitiveness is fierce for attracting these consumers as a consequence. This sort of business environment is perfect for consumers because product creativity and efficient prices come with fair competition. One can check for the following important characteristics when choosing a trading platform:

Speed

It should be a web-based platform with the ability to deliver speed, ensuring ease of use, and the tools needed for traders to succeed.

Low costs

Commissions and other charges should be a matter of concern as these are deducted from your profits.

Options tools

The desktop application should have easy trading and intensive analysis. Option software should have a personalized classification, real-time Greek streaming, and specialized position analysis for existing positions.

It must give and show all the resources that an options trader would like in an efficient way. Some of them could be spread groupings, easy strategy screening, and risk/reward details that are simple to grasp. It must encourage customers to build custom rules and instantly roll up their current options positions. It should be outstanding for the number of settings and depth of choice.

Trading platforms can be built for both novice and experienced options traders. You, as an investor, should expect from your broker to include scanning, P&L analysis, risk analysis, and easy-order management.

3.5 The Broker

Trading profitably allows you to use a brokerage company that aligns with your financial priorities, educational requirements and personal style.

Choosing the right online stockbroker that suits your needs, particularly for new investors, may mean the difference between an exciting new income stream and crushing disappointment.

Although there are no surefire means of guaranteeing returns on investment, a way to ensure your success is met by the selection of the online brokerage that better fits the needs of yours.

Exposure to the capital markets is simple and cheap due to a number of brokers operating online portals. Different online brokers are tailored for a particular category of the customer — from long-term buy-and-hold novices to professional, successful day traders.

Finding the right broker online needs some due diligence to get the best out of your funds. Follow the measures and guidance to pick the right one:

- Know Your Needs

- Narrow the Field

- Look at Brokerage Account Offerings

- Figure Out the Fees

- Know about Online Security and Account Protection

- Trading Commissions

- Test the Broker's Platform

- Provision of Charting Features

- Stock Broker's Quality and Usability

- How Well Does the Stock Broker Educate Its Clients

- Analytical Resources offered by the broker

- Ease of Depositing and Withdrawing Funds

- Customer Service

Margins

In options dealing, "margin" often applies to the cash or assets needed to be deposited with the brokerage company by an option writer as collateral for the obligation of the writer to purchase or sell the underlying security or, in the case of cash-settled options, to compensate the balance of the cash payout if the option is assigned.

For option writers, margin specifications are difficult and not the same for each form of the underlying security. They are subject to change and can differ from one brokerage company to another brokerage company. As they have a major effect on each trade's risk/reward profiles, option writers (whether they be calls or puts alone or as part of several position strategies like spreads, straddles or strangles) can decide the specific margin criteria of their brokerage companies and ensure that if the market turns against them, they are willing to fulfill those specifications.

Margin Requirements Manual

A margins requirements manual for various options strategies has been published by **CBOE**.

Margin Calculator

CBOE has also provided a **useful online tool** that helps to calculate the exact margin requirements for a specific trade.

Margin call

In the case of an unfavorable market movement, margins are needed to guarantee that you will fulfill your future obligations. Margins are payable for option writers only, while buyers of options do not.

An Options margin call is where the broker needs extra cash or stocks to be given by a customer who has written Options. A failure to fulfill a margin call can result in the closing of your Options positions.

How are Margins triggered

A margin call can be triggered for a score of factors, but the most common reasons are:

When a position moves against you, it consequently increases your potential obligation under the Options contract.

The exchange increases the margin requirement against your positions. The exchange reduces the collateral value allowed on your shares deposited as cover.

CHAPTER 4: Financial Leverage and Risk Management

One of the greatest advantages of trading options is financial leverage. In order to increase profits, flexibility is generated by having your assets function harder for you. Leveraging allows a limited volume of money to build the opportunity for greater profits.

To increase potential earnings, financial leverage is typically generated by utilizing the resources of other people. In order to invest in real estate, deposits are used, and firms raise capital to increase activities. The gain of the leverage arises from the improved valuation of the land or the higher income of the business, which enhances the worth of the securities of the stockholders.

However, buying options offers intrinsic financial leverage to the user. Without the need to use borrowed money, you will control the greater amount of shares with the same initial capital by trading in options than if you owned the shares yourself.

Leverage.

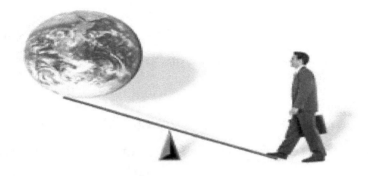

For instance, you might buy 10 IMAX stock shares (hypothetically) priced at $100 per share if you choose to invest $1000. Alternatively, with lots of 100 securities ($2.00 per option), the options contracts could reasonably be priced at $200. You may acquire five options contracts for your commitment of $1 000, increasing your financial leverage by enabling you to own 500 securities instead of only 10.

If the value of such securities improves significantly throughout the option contract, you will wish to purchase the securities that you have the right to purchase at the negotiated price (strike price), which is far cheaper than the market value at that time. If you purchased the ten securities with the $1 000, you would then resell those securities at market value, making a return from a significantly higher amount of shares than the ones you might have owned initially. Obviously, though, you will need to have access to even more money to conduct this transaction in order to buy the securities that your options allow you to buy, and be able to bear the chance of unexpected decline in the stock price until you have the ability to resell your assets.

In this investment, though, the strongest source of financial leverage derives from the assumption that the percentage improvement in the option is proportionately greater than the increase in the underlying share. In order to purchase and sell the securities that your options offer you the ability to own, this leverage often comes without the expense of spending even larger sums of cash.

Let's assume in the previously stated hypothetical transaction that the value of the stock grows from $100 per and reaches $105 per share. The return that this will produce on your $1 000 expenditure would be $50, or a 5 percent raise if you purchased those 10 securities.

A fair calculation, on the other side, is that an improvement from $2.00 to $2.80 per option is the equivalent of the options you might have purchased. This creates an improvement of $400, or 40 percent, for your 500 options. This far higher possible rise is a way that leverage can easily generate by trading options.

However, it is necessary to be mindful that the prospective loss is often greater. A 5% valuation loss on stock may imply a 40 percent value loss on the corresponding options.

In trading options, knowing financial leverage, the gains and costs are very critical. Using leverage will help you to optimize your returns with an effective trading strategy while mitigating the risk.

Advantage of Leverage in Options Trading

The stability and variety they bring, and the broad variety of tactics that can be utilized, are one of the main factors that investors want to trade options. There are, in fact, a variety of methods that may be used either to minimize the danger of taking a position or to minimize the initial expense of taking a position.

It's possible to enter a trade using any of the reduced risk techniques to know precisely what the actual total loss is, which can be really helpful when organizing trades. However, trading in options is generally regarded to be high risk, and substantial losses may be incurred. Obviously, the less likely you are to have disastrous errors, the better you practice, and the more exposure you gain, but even seasoned traders will make mistakes, and it is essential to realize what form of risks you are exposed to.

The idea that you can use leverage to efficiently maximize the value of your resources is a big gain that is frequently stated. For instance, if you purchased $1,000 worth of call options based on Company X stock, then you might expect to earn even bigger money. If the stock's price increased, you must invest the $1,000 directly into the stock.

A disadvantage of Leverage in Options trading

The other side of this, though, in specific regard to the aforementioned case, is if the stock dropped in value or even only stayed the same, your call options could end up useless, and you will lose the whole $1,000. If you had purchased the stocks instead, if Business X went bankrupt, you would just lose half of the $1,000. This demonstrates a big risk, and that you might purchase options to expire worthlessly, suggesting you lose everything you have put in such contracts.

Calculating Leverage to determine how much Leverage you need

Assume that an XYZ company trading at $50 rises to $55 the next trading day. Consequently the $50 strike call options will move up from $2 to $4.50, depicting a gain of $2.50 ($5 x 0.5 = $2.50).

Therefore, the actual options leverage of an option position can be computed by using the following formula:

Options Leverage = (delta equivalent stock price - option price) / option price

Base on the above example: XYZ shares are trading at $50, and its $50 strike price call options have a delta value of 0.5:

Options Leverage = ([$50 x 0.5] - $2) / $2 = 11.5 times

The above options leverage calculation demonstrates that the $50 strike call options of XYZ company incorporate the leverage of an option of 11.5 times. This means that it gives you an opportunity to multiply your profits by 11.5 times. In other words, 11.5 times options leverage compounds your money by 11.5 times.

Options Leverage - Interpretation

In options trading, knowing multiple leverage options is important, since the higher the multiple of leverage options, the greater the chance of losing. In option investing, leverage is a double-edged weapon and risk/reward is proportionate to one another. As a result, the leverage of In The Money options will still be smaller than the leverage of At The Money Options

options and is smaller than the Out Of The Money Options.

Refer to above example where XYZ shares are trading at $50 and its

$50 strike price call options is asking for $2 with a delta value of 0.5

$45 strike price call options is asking for $6 with a delta value of 0.8

$55 strike price call options is asking for $0.10 with a delta value of 0.01

Options Leverage (1) = ([$50 x 0.5] - $2) / $2 = 11.5 times

Options Leverage (2) = ([$50 x 0.8] - $6) / $6 = 5.7 times

Options Leverage (3) = ([$50 x 0.01] - $0.01 / $0.01 = 49 times

As you can see above, the leverage of options on the out of the money $55 strike price call options is significantly greater than the leverage of options on the $45 strike price call options in the money, which also reinforces the teaching that the options that are out of the money are more risky than the options in the money.

While 49 times more benefit is given by the out of the money options, it may also cause 49 times the losses resulting in the elimination of all the capital invested if XYZ business fails to push above its strike price by expiry.

Risk & Money Management

When trading options, correctly controlling the capital and risk exposure is important. Although the risk for any sort of investment is ultimately inevitable, the risk exposure doesn't have to be an issue. The aim is to efficiently control the risk funds; please make sure you are secure with the risk amount being taken and so you are not vulnerable to excessive losses.

It is necessary to use the same principles when controlling the resources as well. Use the money that you can manage to lose while you trade; stop overstretching yourself. As efficient risk and money management is the key to effective trading of options, it is a topic that you really need to learn. Some of the strategies you may, and should, use to handle your exposure to risk and regulate your budget are listed below.

Using Your Trading Plan

A comprehensive trading strategy that sets out rules and criteria for your trading activities is really essential. Helping you control your resources, and your risk exposure is one of the realistic applications of such a plan. Your strategy should provide specifics of the risk level you are confident with and the amount of money you intend to use.

You will prevent one of the biggest mistakes that buyers and traders commit by executing the strategy by just utilizing resources that you have expressly reserved for options trading: utilizing "scared" funds.

You are much less able to make sound choices about your trade while you are investing with capital that you cannot afford to risk or could have put aside for other purposes. Although it's impossible to fully eradicate the emotion inherent with trading options, you just want to be as focused on what you do and why you do.

When emotion takes control, you can tend to lose your attention and are likely to act irrationally. For instance, it might potentially lead you to pursue losses from previous trades that had gone wrong or make purchases that you normally wouldn't do. You can have a lot greater chance at holding your feelings in check if you implement that strategy and stick to managing that financial money.

Equally, the degree of danger that you describe in your strategy should really be adhered to. If you want to make trades with low risk, so there is really no justification why you should start submitting yourself to higher risk levels. Maybe because you have created a few errors and you want to attempt to fix them, it's always enticing to do this, or perhaps you have performed better on certain low-risk transactions and want to start increasing the earnings at a quicker pace.

If you planned to make low-risk transactions, though, then you clearly did so for a reason, and because of the same emotional reasons listed above, there is no sense in putting yourself out of your comfort zone.

Managing Risk with Options Spreads

Options spreads are important and effective instruments in the trading of options. Basically, the spread of an option is where you merge more than one position on options contracts depending on the same underlying security to establish one overall trading position efficiently.

For instance, if you purchased a particular stock's in the money calls and then wrote cheaper on the same stock out of the market calls, then you might have produced a spread known as a bull call spread. If the underlying stock went up in value, purchasing the calls ensures you stand to benefit, but if the market price did not go up, you would lose any or more of the money invested in purchasing them. You will be able to manage any of the original expenses by writing calls on the same stock and thereby reduce the overall sum of money you might lose.

The usage of spreads includes many trading techniques for options, and these spreads are a very helpful way to handle risk. As with the bull call spread example provided above, you may use them to decrease the overall costs of entering a position and to reduce how much money you stand to risk. This suggests that the gains you will earn are theoretically limited, but it decreases the inherent risk.

Spreads may often be used while taking a short position to decrease the risks involved. For instance, if you wrote in the money puts on a stock, you will obtain an initial payout to write certain options, so if the stock fell in value, you will be subject to future losses. If you purchased cheaply out of the money puts as well, so you might have to expend some of the upfront investment. However, you would reduce any possible losses that might trigger a drop in the stock.

As you will see from all of these cases if the market moves in the correct direction for you, it is possible to enter positions that you also stand to prosper, yet you should narrowly restrict any losses you might suffer if the price moves against you. This is why spreads are so commonly used by traders in options; they are superb risk control instruments. There is a broad variety of spreads that can be used to benefit from nearly every market condition.

Managing Risk through Diversification

Diversification is a risk control strategy that is usually employed by investors who use a buy and hold policy to construct a portfolio of stocks. For certain buyers, the underlying concept of diversification is that the allocation of capital through various firms and industries generates a diverse portfolio rather than making so much capital locked up with one single business or industry. In general, a diversified portfolio is perceived to be less risk-exposed than a portfolio that is solely made up of one single form of investment.

Diversification is not necessary in the same manner when it comes to alternatives, but it does have its applications, and you can potentially diversify in a variety of different forms. Although the idea stays essentially the same, you don't want so much of your money allocated to a single type of investment; diversification is done across a number of strategies of options trading.

By using a variety of different tactics, by trading options depending on a number of underlying stocks, and by trading multiple forms of options, you will diversify. Essentially, the principle of utilizing diversification is that you stand to earn money in a variety of forms and with all the trades to be efficient, you are not fully dependent on one specific result.

Managing Risk Using Options Orders

Using the range of different orders that you may place is a reasonably straightforward method of handling risk. There is a range of additional instructions that you can place,

and all of these can assist you in risk control.

For instance, at the moment of implementation, a standard market order would be filled out at the best possible price. This is an absolutely common way to buy and sell options; however, the order can end up being filled at a price that is higher or lower than you expect it to be in a dynamic market. You can prevent purchasing or selling at less desirable rates by utilizing limit orders, where you can specify the minimum and maximum costs at which your order can be filled.

You may also use instructions to automate the exit of a position: whether to lock in gains already earned or to minimize losses on a deal that has not performed well. You can easily monitor at what stage you quit a position by utilizing instructions like the market stop order, the trailing stop order, or the limit stop order.

This can help you to prevent circumstances where you lose out on gains by hanging on to a position for too long or suffer major losses by not closing out rapidly enough in a terrible position.

You will restrict the risk you are subjected to each and every transaction you create by utilizing option orders accordingly.

Money Management and Position Sizing

The management of your money is inextricably related to risk management, and both are equally important. Ultimately, you have a limited amount of cash to use, and it is important to have strict management over the capital expenditure and to guarantee that you do not risk everything and that you finally become unable to do any more transactions.

Using a very basic term known as position sizing is the single best way to handle your capital. Basically, position sizing determines how much of the money you choose to use to enter some given position.

To use position sizing efficiently, in terms of a percentage of your total investment resources, you need to decide how much to spend in each specific transaction. Position sizing is a method of diversification in several respects. You would never be too focused on one particular result by just utilizing a limited percentage of your resources in any one trade. Also, the most effective traders can make transactions that rarely come out terribly; the trick is to ensure that you are not too seriously impacted by the poor ones.

For instance, if in one trade you have 50 percent of your investment resources locked up and it ends up costing you money, then you would actually have spent a large sum of your usable funds. If you prefer to only use 5 % to 10% of your money per trade, then you cannot be wiped out by even a few straight losing deals.

If you are optimistic that in the long term, your trading strategy can work, so you need to be prepared to push through the tough times and still have ample resources to turn it around. Position sizing will assist you in achieving just that.

4.1 Advanced Trading Strategies for Options

The great news is that with options, traders having all skilled levels can learn how to trade the market. Options trading techniques typically utilize momentum metrics such as the Relative Strength Index (RSI) to warn them when market moves are exaggerated, either upside-down or downside-up and are primed for a reversal in the opposing direction.

Also, traders manage to stay longer in trade. It will make them better off to operate overnight being a part of a swing trading plan, as acquired option positions have reduced downside danger.

Option traders use various options strategy, which includes buying or selling one or other options to have either market-neutral or directional views of the underlying asset market.

These often usually use diagrams called option compensation or reward profiles to provide a quick understanding of whether the option plan would payout with a variety of underlying market prices, including the one seen below, on the expiry date.

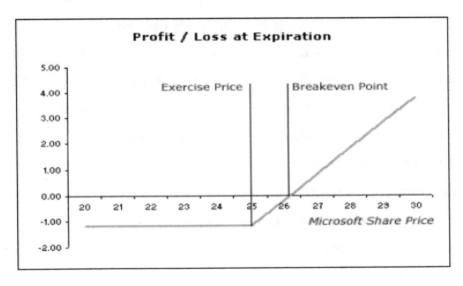

The blue line in this graph indicates how if the demand hits the breakeven stage, the option price begins making revenue at expiration. The position can also indicate a profit before expiry, however, if you can sell the option at a price higher than the purchase price. This is usually the goal when swinging trading the options.

Fortunately, you can understand how to trade options to apply your market opinion for a directional trading strategy such as swing trading. The instructions below illustrate how to use a basic option strategy to swing trade in almost every financial asset sector where options are easily accessible, such as purchasing a call or put option.

Select an Asset

The first phase in swing trading with options is to pick an underlying commodity for trade that you have established as an incentive to sell. Swing traders would also track different equity markets in order to provide a better probability of having a successful trading setup. In picking an asset, search for equity price that is prone to a downturn as defined by a measure of momentum, such as the RSI. A specific measure is a range-bound oscillator that indicates an overbought position when its cost is over 70 or oversold position when it's worth is below 30.

Look to sell a market at RSI rates over 70 and purchase it at rates below 30

When you like any more accurate swing trading indications from the RSI, you should wait before you see something occurring called price-RSI variance, which implies that the market price rises briskly, such as reaching a new peak, but the RSI does not. That's an even stronger swing trading warning that an impending recession is coming to the market.

Select a Direction

For example, If you have established demand and used your chosen method of demand research to identify a trading chance with a reasonable reward/risk ratio of two or more to one, whether technical and/or fundamental, then you may feel better utilizing call and/or put options to take a directional market view of the underlying commodity.

For e.g., if you think the demand would improve, you'd have a call option to go on the market for a long period. With restricted downside risk and limitless upside potential for the underlying market, you want to trade.

Instead, if your point of view was that the market would fall, instead, you would buy a put option, again with a restricted risk of the downside and unlimited potential for upside.

The payoff profiles shown for long call and put options at expiry shows how your losses are restricted to the premium Paid if it turns out that your directional perception is wrong. In addition, possible profits on an option position are infinite and

begin to accumulate past the breakeven point where the profits on the position go beyond the bonus paid.

Call Option

Put Option

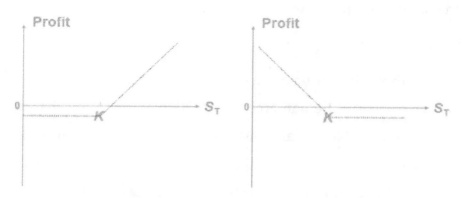

Call and put option payoff profiles with a strike price of K. Source: Surlytrader.com

Choose a Strike Price

An option's strike price aids in determining its price. The more appealing an option's strike price is in relation to the current market cost for the underlying asset, the more it will charge. Also, the longer time frame a particular strike price option has until expiry, the more it will be expensive.

When strike rates are higher than the prevalent sector, it is assumed that they are either "in the pocket." An option with an ITM strike price has "intrinsic value," corresponding to the change between the normal market price (for the delivery date of the option) and the strike price. When the strike price of an option is right on the prevailing market, it's "at the cash" or ATM, and when it is "out of cash," or OTM, at a worse level than the prevailing market. There is no inherent interest in both the OTM and ATM products.

Many swing traders are trying to take advantage of reasonably short-term price fluctuations in a sector, and they are likely to choose an OTM opportunity as they expect ITM to go fast, thus enabling them to sell it back. It is because options have time value along with the intrinsic value, and as time grows towards expiration, the time value declines increasingly. This inspires a swing trader to sell back an option that they bought when a reasonable profit represents itself at the first opportunity.

Agree on an Expiration Date

Selecting an expiry date would represent, in part, how long you believe it would take the underlying market to achieve your target price. You'll need to select a shorter-term option if you suppose the transfer would be a longer-term option, especially if you assume it could take more time.

For a swing trader, you simply don't want to have an option that dies so early because it could end up being useless at expiration. On the other side, owing to the comparatively high cost, you do not intend to purchase an option with an expiry date so long in the future.

Often swing traders would pick options or calls for about one month on the near-future market if it is more than a month out since this normally allows them ample room to work out before expiry.

Time Your Entry

The timing of trading entries is usually completed using technical evaluation. Since swing traders deal both with patterns and with adjustments to such patterns, they first must recognize, if any, the dominant pattern in the commodity they are looking at.

Swing traders would go for a remedial pullback while trading with the trend to create a position in trend direction. If the pullback appears to be losing steam, as shown by an RSI level in over-bought or over-sold range, preferably indicating price deviation, they will believe the time to enter the market is ripe.

Carry Out Your Trade

When the time has come for the trade, it's time to proceed according to the trading schedule. For example, if the global trend is above average, you could buy an OTM call option or an OTM put option if the marketplace is downward.

It's always crucial to note that the way you deal is just as critical as the point at which you sell, so make sure you select the best broker as your business companion. Transaction costs can certainly add up over a period, including handling spreads and fees if you regularly trade as a swing dealer.

Manage the Position

You run the risk of failure after you have conducted trade and have a choice, but because you bought an option, the liability would be restricted to the price you paid for it. You may always need to track the underlying demand to better handle the option trade. If you buy an OTM share, you will decide to sell it until the underlying market hits the price of the strike, and it is ATM. If the time value rises, that would also rise in the option of selecting an extra prime.

The decay of time would be struggling with potential gains occurring for each day an option approaches its expiry date. This suggests that at the earliest moment possible, you'll want to sell back the option position to prevent making a deal centered on a perception that directionally seemed risk value due to premature deterioration over time. If the market still seems like your trade would finally pan out, but the short-term change you planned to capitalize on and disastrous to materialize will allow it more time period to come to fruition.

It may be achieved by conducting a calendar roll-out swap that includes selling back your own near-term option and purchasing a longer-term option at a similar strike price. This avoids you from having losses as their expiration approaches because of the greatly increasing time decline on near-money options.

Married Put

An investor purchases an asset in a married put strategy and, at the same time, purchases put options on an equal amount of securities. The buyer of the put option is entitled to sell the stock at the strike price, and the value of each contract is 100 shares.

When keeping a stock, an investor can opt to use this strategy as a way to minimize their downside risk. For instance, suppose an investor buys 100 stock shares and simultaneously buys one put option. In the case of a significant shift in the market price, this approach could be beneficial to this investor since they are shielded from the downside. Around the same moment, if the asset rises in value, the investor will be able to participate in any possibility of upside. The main drawback to this approach is that the investor sacrifices the balance of the premium charged on the put option if the stock does not decrease in value.

Long Butterfly

Butterfly spread options are made up of 2 vertical spreads with a similar strike price. In other terms, an opening position where options (either calls or puts) are acquired (or sold) at 3 separate strike rates includes butterfly options. The method in which these options are produced renders the butterfly a position of both limited losses and limited benefits.

It is possible to build the Long Butterfly spread option using either all call options or all put options. A Long Butterfly formed using call options would work like one generated using put options due to put-call parity. In other terms, it doesn't really matter if you make your Long Butterfly using calls or puts.

Short Iron Condor Strategy

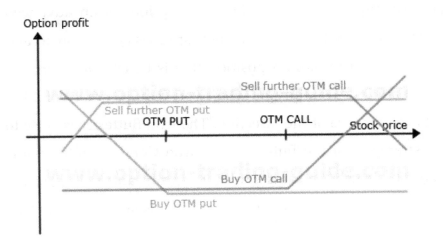

An advanced options trading technique that utilizes a mixture of two vertical spreads is the Iron Condor strategy. At strike prices that are greater than the current price of the underlying stock, a call spread is opened, and a put spread is opened at strike prices, which are lower than the current price.

For volatile stocks, the Short Iron Condor technique is used. It is created by opening up a bullish out-of-the-money (OTM) call spread, and a bearish out-of-the-money (OTM) put spread. You purchase an OTM call, and you sell an extra OTM call. Then you purchase an OTM put then sell an OTM put, which is an extra OTM. This causes a scenario of debit spread, whereby when you open the position, you need to compensate for the difference in premiums.

Long Iron Butterfly Options

The technique of the Iron Butterfly options is an advanced options strategy that uses 2 vertical spreads (1 call spread and 1 put spread) to build a position that is beneficial when you anticipate low volatility or when you require great volatility but are unaware of the direction. The Iron Butterfly is close to the strategies of the Butterfly and Iron Condor, as the name suggests. It has the same profile for-profit and risk as to the Butterfly but uses a mix of option spreads similar to the Iron Condor.

The most widely used variant of the Iron Butterfly is the Long Iron Butterfly option. They are ideal for stocks that would not change significantly (low volatility).

4.2 Avoid common beginner mistakes

You are not forced to buy or to sell while trading options. You actually have the right to trade two kinds of stock options instead: puts and calls. Participants in new options are enthusiastic about the advantage's participants earn and make errors. To avoid errors, you must read about the mistakes made by the option traders.

Starting too Big

Starting too big is the first error most novice options traders make. Start dealing with smaller positions in the business. To start your options trading experience on the right foot, sell a limited number of shares at a time.

Using only one Strategy

Options traders usually start off by trading long and short. Although you could achieve success using this technique, it should not be the only approach you use. Options trading gives you too many innovative options for trading strategy. As a novice, connect with what works for you while studying new techniques simultaneously. Then, this common error that new options traders make can be avoided.

Illogical Expiration Date

Novice traders of options often struggle to realize the expiration's power. Although you have various choices for your expiry date, not all of them are produced equally. You ought to get an attitude first in order to pick the right expiration date for you. Question yourself how long you expect the trade is going to take. Evaluate liquidity. Do not make a premature call about your expiration date to prosper as a novice options trader.

Thinking cheaper is beneficial

By purchasing out-of-the-money, several start-up options traders lose out. Through purchasing out-of-the-money, you hold the premium on an option cheap. When they are told not to go too big, several new buyers opt for this approach. When engaged in options trading, strive to make good choices, not simply cheap choices.

Increasing the number of trades to make up for Losses

Finally, to recoup early losses as an options investor, stay away from doubling up. Once investors like you start trading options, they find it challenging to control losses and leap into trying to catch up. They do that by doubling up in an effort to reduce their cost structure per deal. While this may happen when doubling up, it typically does not. New option traders, instead, end up exacerbating their risk. Close failed trades instead of attempting to solve problems that have already damaged you and your money. When you understand when to close trades, you move a step closer to transitioning from a novice to a good option investor.

Drawdown

During a particular period, a drawdown is a peak-to-trough fall. The percentage between the high and the following low is generally quoted as a drawdown. When a trading account has $10,000 in it, then before going up over $10,000, the assets decrease to $9,000, so the trading account has seen a 10 percent drawdown.

Drawdowns are relevant for calculating the historical risk of various assets, evaluating the performance of investments or tracking the success of personal trading.

As long as the price stays below the top, a drawdown remains in place. In the above case, once the account goes up above $10,000, we don't realize the drawdown is just 10 percent. The drawdown is registered until the account goes up over $10,000.

This way of tracking drawdowns is beneficial since once a new high emerges, a low can't be calculated. As long as the price or value stays below the old rate, a smaller trough might arise that would raise the amount of drawdown.

Draw-downs help assess the financial risk of an investment. The Sterling ratios provide drawdowns to equate the potential benefit of security to its risk.

Although we try our utmost to handle transactions to avoid losers, losses are inevitable. Our aim, as traders, is to reduce the extent and severity of these losses.

Because losses influence the valuation of your investments, which in turn affects your future purchase power, therefore, keeping losses in check is crucial.

Keeping small positions, generating more activities to make the possibilities play out, and uncorrelated trading products are some of the keys to reducing drawdowns.

Time to Recover a Drawdown

While the scale of drawdowns is a risk determination factor, the period it takes to recover a drawdown is also a factor. Not all assets behave equally. Some recuperate better than most. To recover the loss created by a 10 percent drawdown in one hedge fund or trader's account could take years. On the other side, in a short period of time, another hedge fund or investor could very rapidly regain losses, driving the account to peak value. Therefore, drawdowns can often be viewed in light of how long the transaction or fund has usually taken to recover the loss.

Example of a Drawdown

Suppose a trader agrees to purchase $100 of Apple stock. The price increases to $110 (peak) but then decline to $80 (trough) rapidly and then climbs again to $110.

The stock high was $110, and the low was $80. $30 / $110 = 27.3% is the drawdown.

This means that a drawdown is not inherently equivalent to a loss. The stock drawdown was 27.3%, but while the stock was at $80, the trader will display an unrealized loss of 20 percent. This is since, in terms of their buying price ($100 in this case), most traders perceive losses and not the peak price the investment multiplied after entry.

The price then rallies to $120 (peak), continuing with the scenario, and then drops down to $105 before rallying to $125.

The latest peak is currently $120, and $105 for the newest low. This is a drawdown of $15, or $15 / $120 = 12.5%.

How to deal with Drawdowns

Drawdown in trading is an essential part of the method of trading and is of serious importance to traders, particularly beginners. The reality that 100 percent of profit dealing does not occur. Losses follow all, including the most seasoned, with profits. In addition, drawdowns are deemed a very natural part of each trader's trades. This trend is acknowledged by some individuals, and others are indignant towards this. As a consequence, traders, under the control of feelings, lose major ones. Probably, that's why the issue of drawdowns and how a trader can act is worth discussing.

Reasons for drawdowns in trading

The psychology of trading is the most popular explanation for drawdowns in trading. It is also the mental condition that allows drawdowns to emerge, and perhaps, how well a trader is able to communicate with emotions. Gambling, greed, the ability to boost prices and win back losses can affect the outcome. First of all, as those feelings emerge, a trader must know how to control himself and fight. Otherwise, he would lead to a drawdown himself.

The absence of a functional trade mechanism or successful guidelines for entry is another explanation for a drawdown.

This is the second primary explanation for drawdowns of the trader. Intuitive trading takes place, of course, but only if it's founded on several years of trial, error and success experiences. This is not adopted by all, especially inexperienced traders, as experience demonstrates. Beginners are great at taking up a strategy for trading, learning to work with it and adapting it to trading steadily. They need to handle the discipline problem extremely well. Otherwise, drawdowns would be difficult to prevent.

One of the most substantial factors for the appearance of drawdowns is market developments. Usually, the nature of the economy is volatile and unforeseeable. No one should underestimate the market's uncertainty. And if the findings have been optimistic for a long period of time, drawdowns cannot be excluded. They arise as a consequence of price shifts and, as a consequence, the inefficiency of the trading approach. All of this suggests that considering the very market shifts that lead to the drawdowns, the investor has to modify the preferred approach. This is, after all, an entirely normal circumstance. If the market has evolved, then the trading strategy must adapt.

The natural occurrence of drawdowns can be avoided by risk control since this is attributed to the lack of self-discipline, anger management and the development of a determination to recover losses. It is still necessary to deal with your feelings in time and note that without some drawdowns, there is no trading.

Recommendations for drawdowns in trading

Given below are the methods and ways to manage and control drawdowns in trading.

You must remember one important thing that due to the distinctive traits of each individual, each person will have to look for ways to adapt to these recommendations.

Exits

When it comes to drawdowns, we concentrate on our emotionality and responses. A perfect way is to take a time-out and rest your minds from trading. Taking a break is going to really ideally place things in order. Understand, you're not going to lose much in a couple of hours, which is time to calm off. After all, a number of wonderful prospects are always waiting for you; just losing one or two carry no meanings and shall have no impact on your performance. It's better to live with the heat of passion than to risk all the capital.

Self-discipline

Next, we're talking about self-discipline that helps build a trader's diary. This is popular and the easiest and efficient approach. Start registering new deals and outcomes after relaxing and dealing with emotions. You should read up on your errors. You should not be lazy here, knowing that the game is worth the flame and any transaction carefully documented would in the future show the correct direction. This is a waste of time; many people say, because they don't need a diary at all. It is not like that at all, because even trading masters have been maintaining their diaries for years. When the trader falls further and further into a drawdown, it is extremely necessary to maintain a journal.

Manage Stress

The issue of the trader's psychology determines a process, the physical load, which is not always normal, but successful. This is an outstanding strategy for minimizing steam in reaction to each oversight or failure, attempt physical workouts. To expel the unwanted feelings and ideas, others actually have a couple of squats or push-ups. Thus, from the chaotic state, the trader lets himself out. Also, those who do not have the chance to participate in physical exercises for different reasons might try respiratory equipment. Starting trading with a cold head is still the main thing.

Example of dealing with drawdown

There are a variety of ways to help reduce some of the risks to the portfolio of an active trader, and when faced with drawdowns, the top strategies are listed below.

If the investment is in long stock, the first strategy may be carried out. Through selling an out-of-the-money call, the benefit opportunity has been limited, which certainly might put certain investors off. Costs per equity have, however, been decreased.

You have simply reduced the price per share down to $18 a share by purchasing 100 XYZ securities for $20 a share and offering a call on those securities for $2, minimizing the risk in the transaction and converting a buy-and-hope plan into trading with high chance options.

At best, 45-60 days before expiration, you should look at a 30-delta call. That would offer a large sum of credit and also have a 70 % chance of not breaching the call, enabling the investor to roll out the request as time passes and receive even further cash, thereby lowering the trade's cost base.

Furthermore, if you sell a spread of out-of-the-money, and the share price moves in the opposite direction and is in the money now, you might sell the opposing spread.

So this will simply sell a call spread against it if the fund has a short put spread. It generates an iron condor transaction by doing this, but it still helps the trader to bring in an extra trading credit. When you sold a two-dollar wide put spread for fifty cents, then the risk for the initial contract was $150.

You brought in $30 in credit and decreased the trade risk down to $120 by selling the competing call spread for 30 cents. It won't save a deal that's gone bad, though some of the danger will be mitigated.

If both the short and long legs of the trade are in the money on at least three straight trading days, you will apply this adjustment.

The last strategy is to roll out the spread in time. If it's not turned lucrative by 30 days or so before expiration has come, you can choose for this.

This helps you to usually draw in extra credits by rolling out of time and offers your trade 1-2 additional months to turn successful. In order to be right, the aim here is to take in more cash, reduce risk and improve time.

While trading options enable a trader to generate a huge chance of benefit, there is still a risk something might go wrong. Before initiating the trade, getting a strategy in place is the secret. It would help you transact more easily than just purchasing and wishing for the best, by holding the risk per transaction minimal and getting a documented exit goal and adjustment trigger.

When to exit an options trade

It will also support to be much more successful, but it is not important to quit trades early to be profitable. It is also a smart decision to close option positions, especially when they hit 50 percent or another fraction of the max benefit. This isn't known to most traders, so it sounds like a terrible plan. Many traders agree that closing a position at half of the benefit decreases a strategy's total profitability because you get less cash. While it may appear like this is the case, it really is not. It is because closing trades early at a lower benefit generally boosts efficiency and is a really smart idea.

Guaranteed Winners

It will be a guaranteed gain if you leave a trade early for less than max profit. When the position is still at 50 percent of the full value, if you close it, it is a lucrative transaction. This indicates you've made a profit. It is not an assured benefit if you do not close it early. The position will also switch around to become a losing position. Sometimes, keeping trade and aiming to hit maximum profit is not worth the risk. This implies early closing trades would potentially boost your win rate, so as soon as they hit your benefit objective, you need to close trades and don't let them turn into losses.

More Trades

You would be prepared to enter into fresh trading faster if you close positions early. This suggests that with any transaction, you allocate funds for a shorter amount of time. This also increases the number of trades that you can enter into. Premium trading in high-risk options is mostly about the accuracy and having as many transactions as possible. This is precisely what early closing positions would allow. In an expiration loop, you would be ready to take profits sooner and launch fresh ones quicker, thereby trading more in total.

Assignment Risk

You will most likely be allocated far fewer stocks if you want to leave trades early. The less time an option has before its expiry, the more probable it is to be exercised. In the last week of an expiry period, about 80 percent of options are exercised. This is because, in the last week, only a tiny extrinsic time value exists. Therefore, closing out an option contract and then buying the shares would not be more lucrative.

Early closure of options positions would also avoid the last days/weeks of an expiry period and therefore reduce the chance of being assigned. This, without any doubt, is a really positive thing, especially for smaller account traders, who might have difficulty managing an assignment.

Gamma Risk

The Greek Gamma option calculates Delta's rate of shift for each $1 transfer in the underlying. Gamma often varies all the time, much as the price of your option or the underlying. The closest you come to expiration, Gamma rises. What this suggests is that the value of the option contract becomes even more susceptible to market fluctuations in the underlying as you move near to expiration. In the expiration period, Delta can adjust much faster than it did earlier. This suggests that losing/winning chance can, therefore, be more unpredictable. The value of the option contract can increase/decrease far more than earlier in the expiration cycle for every $1 change in the underlying price. For short positions, Gamma is negative, and for long positions, positive. This suggests that the underlying short positions lose more and more of their worth on any $1 shift. For every move, long positions, on the other side, lose less and less. Gamma risk of directional risk, particularly in the last weeks of an expiration period, is something that an option trader should certainly be aware of.

This means that the closest you come to expiration, the more cash you will risk with a slight step in the underlying and the closest you get to expiration, the larger the Gamma rises. You would risk even more from a few dollar shifts in the underlying price prior to expiration (with a high Gamma) than early in the expiration period. This is also the rationale why selling short-term options is not generally quite pleasant, even though time decay is maximum in the last week before expiration.

A Trading Routine Is Vital To Your Success

Habit is what really defines our progress or failure, inclusive of trading in every initiative. So, how do we build the kind of behaviors that will contribute to successful trading for us?

A routine is a remedy.

What are you thinking about when you contemplate your normal trading routine? Have you ever got one? You know that all experts, whether they recognize it or not, have specific procedures and special routines. These schedules and rituals are followed as clockwork, all from food, workout, sleep, and meditation.

After a successful regular trading pattern has become an

entrenched practice, it has basically become part of you, and you practically become an 'auto-pilot.'

The power of daily trading routines

You could not make it without a regular trading schedule.

It's not only about making a trading schedule; it's about what you're doing from the moment you wake up to the moment you sleep. It's just part of your everyday trading routine.

A regular routine has been established by experienced traders. This enables them to maximize their capacity to trade efficiently and effectively. What does it look like here? Well, it will certainly differ from one trader to another, but it will be common for all of the components of a normal trading routine: Get a good night's sleep, ideally 7 to 8 hours.

A good and nourishing breakfast is a must.

Analyze the **daily chart trend** of the markets you want to trade at the start of the week.

Find out the **key horizontal support and resistance levels** at the start of the trading week.

Study and analyze your charts of interest daily in the morning. Look for **price action signals** that match with the daily chart trend and support or resistance levels.

Look at your favorite markets soon after the **New York close**. Try to look and spot for visible and potent price action that could have a significant impact on the trend.

If a trading signal compliments your trading plan criteria, take a position and go to sleep till the next morning. If you are unable to spot any lucrative trade, then move away from the screen and take rest till tomorrow morning.

If a trade has not been closed and it is still open, review it in the morning and only notice what has happened, unless there is an apparent, reasonable justification to do so, do not take any action. You should just observe, recall, set up, and forget much of the time.

The above, though brief and plain, is an instance of a smart trading routine. The main point to remember in the above process is that we don't waste any time reviewing or entering transactions on the market. Instead, we treat the business the same way and approximately every day at the same time, because our minds are prepared to start converting this low-maintenance, easy routine and trading treat into a constructive trading habit.

It is important that you establish your own trading pattern, one that makes sense in your everyday life and schedule. For every trader, the same routine would certainly not work.

The lifestyle of an 'end-of-day' trading routine

Not only will trading boost your trading in an end-of-day way, but it will also enable you to have a happier life and enjoy the 'fruits' of trading.

Like the one mentioned above, the trading pattern that many effective traders follow helps us to spend a lot of time of a day away from the charts. After all, having a normal 9 to 5 monotonous, time-consuming career is not part of the reason most of us get into trading, right? So, if you still want independence, you need to trade in an end-of-the-day way.

The science behind routines

A game-changer for imagination is an everyday activity. It keeps tasks continuously simmering in the subconscious, among other items, and studies demonstrate how strong the unconscious mind is, allowing us to make smarter choices than active thinking.

Making a schedule tends to make sure you perform stuff correctly. Not only does a routine benefit you instinctively since it holds you in-tune and closely connected to the most critical tasks you need to do every day (such as reviewing the charts), thereby getting you great at them (think practice), but it would also give you the strongest opportunities to effectively execute

your trading strategy and follow your market participation rules.

Bottom line

Trading is about autonomy, so don't become a hostage to your charts and the markets. Probably one of the trickiest issues traders have to figure out way too much by trial and error is that they must first understand that the only factor they can manage is themselves in order to attain the sort of trading lifestyle they dream of. Spending more time studying and analyzing your charts does not suggest that you would be a successful trader. A laid-back, comfortable and minimalist sort of routine is the trading routine needed to become a good trader who does not over-trade and get sentimental over-trading.

CHAPTER 5: The Benefits of Technical Analysis in Options Trading

Technical analysis is an art that capitalizes on the study of price charts (minute-based, hourly, daily, weekly, monthly or yearly). The underlying basis of this technique is that all markets trend. Why? This is because the prices during their daily undulation-and-fluctuation-phase hit or attain certain highs and lows. These highs and lows of any stock or commodity are then plotted on a chart. The prices, after being plotted, never surface up in a helter-skelter manner on a graph chart.

These prices, when plotted, take the form of a wave. This wavy form is a classic result of prominent crests (highs) and troughs (lows). Eventually, these highs and lows create identifiable points on the chart. These points can be easily joined by a line which is then studied and analyzed for the identification of future price trend and forecasting of price targets. Besides, this technique helps you to timely identify the buying or selling opportunities and thus offers excellent opening and exit points.

5.1 History of Technical Analysis

We shall briefly review the work and contribution of renowned personalities towards the development and creation of a fabulous technique of Technical Analysis.

Charles Henry Dow

Dow is accredited with the invention of the Dow Jones Industrial Index. Besides, he also has the honor of establishing the renowned "The Wall Street Journal," which has now become a financial benchmark for all financial papers.

Dow would record the highs and lows of Index on a daily, weekly, and monthly basis as he did not have the liberty and facility of recording short-term data on the lines as is being conveniently carried out by modern electronic trading software.

Assumptions of Dow Theory

Charles Dow advocated three primary tenets of his theory for analysis of market price and for making future projections or forecasts.

Market Prices Progress in three trends

The first assumption states prices progress in three forms simultaneously. These forms are described as Primary, Secondary, and Minor trends of the price movement. The prior knowledge of the kind or trend of the market price assists a trader to work out a realistic profit-objective and evade early market exit.

Price discounts all

"Price discounts all" means that the market price at which buyers and sellers concur to enter into a trade is a price that has weathered the brunt of all relevant (positive or negative) information presently available to market participants. This information could vary from new economic fundamental data to new developing events, stories, regional conflicts, central banks' initiatives, and policies, etc. Besides, this final price is also reflective of the current emotional and financial status of the participants. Any new information or contradictory information is efficiently "discounted" by the market participants, and the final price tends to portray the current information level and sentiment status of the participants.

History repeats itself

Technical analysis is described as the study and analysis of past price trends to predict and forecast future price movements and trends. Technical analysis of charts is an art used to detect patterns in price movements. These price patterns are then used to predict future market behavior and price targets.

You must understand and remember that the market is not just several shares of various companies exhibiting different price movements. In reality, a market is a collection of human beings who, based on their knowledge, perception, and financial strength, are responsible for the movement of the price in different directions. It is the demand or supply emanating from the people that make the market depict a specific behavior or trend. This essentially shifts the price!

You will be wrong in your assessment if you think that the sole reason behind a positive movement in the stock price of a company is the significant gains in last year's profits. The price of the stock goes up because profit news is conceived positively by the market participants, and consequently, they jump in with their funds to buy that stock. The human beings demand stoked by specific factors propels upward movement in prices. This is a very critical concept in your knowledge of technical analysis.

Human psychology remains constant and manages to respond to related situations identically. The study and analysis of the past market behavior at turning points are incredibly beneficial and advantageous in the identification of specific price patterns for the development of an understanding of the market's most probable future reaction. Hence, technical analysis assumes that people will persist in doing the same blunders that they did in the past. Human Being relationships are incredibly complicated. The markets, as explained above, reflect people in action, never duplicating their presentation exactly. Still, the recurrence of identical features is necessary to make it easier for market watchers to recognize notable junctions or turning points.

Technical analysis banks on the study of market action, which in turn is contingent upon the study of human psychology. Different chart patterns have established their authenticity as a result of the review of their effectiveness in all types of markets. These patterns continue to appear on charts with a regular frequency depending on the particular trend of the market. These patterns reveal the bullish or bearish psychology of the market participants. The past utility of these price patterns in generating excellent trading profits makes them viable and tenable for future decision making. Hence the key to knowing the future lies in the analysis of the past, or the future is a mere mirror image of the past.

Market Trend and Types

Dow Theory helps in:

Identifying the existence of a trend

Deciphering the direction of the trend

Classifying the phase of the trend

A trend can be identified by merely joining the two points with the help of a line and then extending that line to see if it meets other points to establish its validity.

If the market is registering higher highs and lows, then the upward slanting line is drawn, which reflects the positive or bullish trend in the market. On the contrary, if the market is making lower highs and lows, then a downward slanting line tells about the negative or bearish trend of the market.

Movement of prices from a trough or bottom to crest or a peak is categorized as a rally, while the downside movement from a peak to bottom is defined as a sell-off in the market. The diagram below demonstrates the upward and downward trends with associated rallies and sell-offs, and vice versa.

A market trend is characterized by the presence of three intermittent trends or phases:

Major or Primary Trend or Phase

The core job of a technical analyst is to identify the major direction or long-term trend of the market with the help of different price patterns and tools. This is typically the most critical aspect of technical analysis because it enables the trader to ensure the optimal ride of the wavelength, which translates into the maximization of trade profit. The long term trend usually lasts for one to three years with some variations.

Secondary Trend or Phase

Sell-off or corrections or retracements in the primary trend defines the secondary trend of the market. If the underlying trend is bullish, then any erosion in prices marked by price movement in the opposite direction of the prime trend is classified as a market correction or retracement in the prime trend.

On the contrary, markets in primary bearish or downward trend shall exhibit upward corrective or secondary bullish trends. The secondary trend comparatively has a short time span of three weeks to three months. The technical analyst makes use of the Fibonacci retracement tool to work out the correction or retracement in a given market.

Minor or Consolidative Trend or Phase

The last phase is characterized by the development of minor trends resulting from small corrections within the secondary trend. The direction of prices during the minor trend is always against the direction of the secondary trend. This is typically one of the most tedious phases, and ignorant and hasty traders tend to lose a lot of money in this phase because of choppy price behavior.

However, a technical analyst who is aware of the bigger picture either avoids trading during this phase of the market or keeps his financial commitment minimal. This is because excessive trading in this phase can result in distraction, and you can ultimately be deprived of enjoying the lucrative monetary benefits of major trends.

5.2 Fibonacci Retracement

Fibonacci identified the sequence of numbers that were translated into mathematical relationships and subsequently converted into ratios. These ratios are applied to calculate the approximate length of corrective waves. Fibonacci retracement works by applying the following ratios/percentages to the value arrived at by measuring the distance between a peak or crest and a trough or bottom:

23.6% or 0.236

33% or 0.382

50% or 0.50

61.8% or .618 or 66%

100% (sometimes the markets retrace the total length of the preceding wave)

The identification of retracement levels facilitates the identification of support and resistance levels. This is usually done by drawing horizontal lines at each peak or retracement level. An efficient trader shall use these support and resistance levels to maximize trade profits by astutely defining his entry and exit points.

5.3 Characteristics of technical analysis

The salient characteristics of technical analysis are:

The primary feature of technical analysis requires the usage of price and volume adjustment formulas and trading laws, such as moving averages, RSI, regressions, business cycles, and intraday market trend trends, stock market fluctuations, or chart trend identification.

Unlike fundamental analysis that takes into consideration the company fact market, currency, or commodity, technical analysis measures price, volume, and related market statistics.

Finally, technical analysis is commonly used by traders and financial professionals and is also utilized by aggressive day traders, pit traders, and market makers.

5.4 Types of charts

There are three types of charts that are more commonly used in technical analysis. These are:

Japanese Candlestick Charts

Throughout the 17th century, the Japanese started using scientific analyzes to exchange grains. Although this early iteration of the theoretical review differs from Charles Dow's US iteration introduced about 1900, much of the basic concepts were quite similar:

The "what" (price action) is more important than the "why" (news, earnings, and so on).

All known information is reflected in the price.

Buyers and sellers move markets based on expectations and emotions (fear and greed).

Markets fluctuate.

The actual price may not reflect the underlying value.

Formation of Candlesticks

In order to construct a chart of a candlestick, you must provide a collection of data that includes accessible, large, low and near values for each time frame you want to view. The hollow or loaded candlestick part is called "the core" (also known as "the true core"). The long thin lines above and below the body reflect the high/low scale, which is regarded as "shadows" (also regarded as "wicks" which "tails"). The high is marked by the peak of the upper shadow and the low by the lower shadow's edge. If the stock closes over its starting price, a hollow candlestick will be drawn. The body bottom reflects the price of the opening, and the body top reflects the price of the closure. If the stock ends below the opening price, the top of the body is illustrated with a loaded candlestick reflecting the opening

price and the bottom of the body showing the closing price.

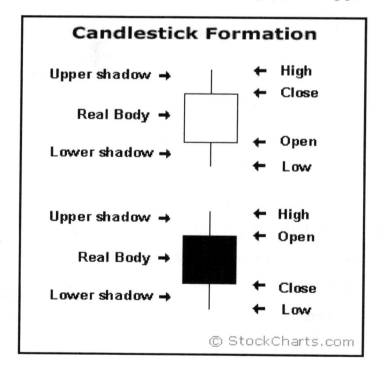

5.5 Hollow candlesticks patterns

Long and Short Bodies

In fact, the longer the body becomes, the more severe the desire to purchase or sell. In comparison, the small candlesticks show no change in prices and reflect consolidation.

Although long white candlesticks are usually bullish, their place within the wider technical picture depends greatly. Long white candlesticks will label a possible tipping point or degree of assistance after sustained decreases. When after a long advance, the buying is too violent, it may contribute to unnecessary bullishness.

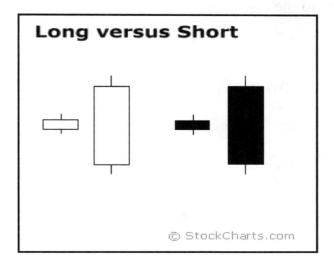

The bigger the black candlestick is, the farther down the open the closure is. This suggests a major drop in rates from the free, yet hostile sellers. A long black candlestick can foreshadow a turning point after a long advance, or mark a future level of resistance. A long black candlestick may indicate panic, or capitulation, after a long decline.

Long and Short Shadows

On candlesticks, the upper and lower shadows will provide useful trading session detail. Upper shadows represent the session low with high and lower shadows. Short shadowed candlesticks suggest that much of the trading activity was contained to the open and close. Long shadowed candlesticks show that prices went well past the open and close.

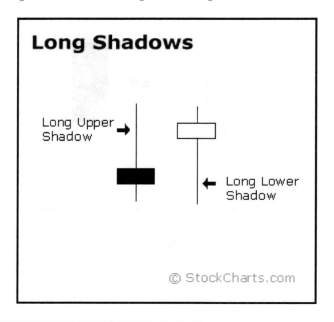

Candlesticks with a long upper shadow and a shorter lower shadow indicate buyers dominated during the session, bidding higher prices, but sellers eventually forced down prices from their highs. This clear comparison of high and low closeness culminated in a long upper shadow. In comparison, candlesticks with long lower shadows and short upper shadows suggest sellers prevailed throughout the session, pushing down costs. Nevertheless, buyers subsequently resurfaced to offer prices higher by the end of the session, along with lower shadow generated by the fast close.

Tall upper shadowed candlesticks, large lower shadow, and tiny actual body are known as spinning tops. One long shadow is a reverse of sorts; spinning tops are indeterminate. The tiny actual body (whether hollow or filled) reveals no change from open to near, and the shadows suggest that during the session, both bears and bulls were involved.

Doji

Doji represents an important type of candlestick, providing information both on their own and as elements of several key forms. When a security's open and close are nearly identical, Doji type, the duration of the upper and lower shadows will differ, with a cross, inverted triangle or plus sign appearing like the resulting candlestick. Together, neutral trends are doji. The previous market behavior and potential evidence form the foundation of every bullish or bearish bias. The term "Doji" applies to the singular as well as the plural form.

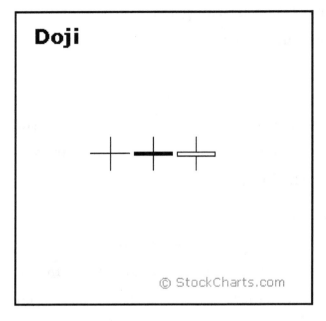

A dog's relevance depends on the previous pattern or the candlesticks before it. A Doji indicates after an advance that the purchasing momentum is starting to diminish. A Doji indicates after a decline that the sales pressure is starting to decrease.

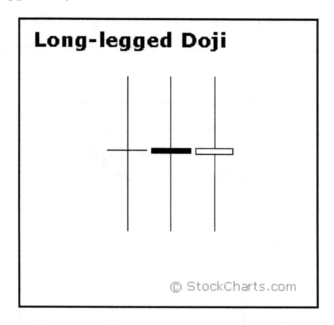

Long-legged Doji has long shadows, upper and lower, which are almost identical in length. This Doji represents a significant amount of business indecision. Long-legged Doji show rates exchanged both above and below the opening stage of the session but were practically closed even with the free. The final product, despite a whole bunch of shouting and crying, shows no improvement from the original available.

Dragonfly Doji and Gravestone Doji

When the open, high, and close are equal, the Dragonfly Doji is formed, and the low creates a long, lower shadow. Owing to the absence of an upper shadow, the resultant candlestick appears like a "T" Dragonfly Doji shows trade was controlled by sellers and pushed prices down throughout the session. By the end of the day, investors resurfaced and moved prices down to the day high and opening stage.

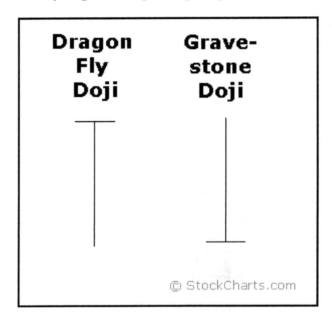

A dragonfly doji's reversal effects rely on prior market behavior and potential confirmation. The long lower shadow is indicative of purchasing demand, but the low shows that there are already plenty of sellers lingering. If the open, short, and close are similar, the Gravestone Doji type and the high produces a long upper shadow. Despite the absence of a lower eye, the resultant candlestick appears like an upside-down "T" Gravestone Doji suggests investors have controlled dealing and pushed higher prices throughout the session. However, sellers resurfaced and pushed prices back to opening and low session levels by the end of the session. As with the dragon fly doji and other candlesticks, Gravestone doji's reversal effects depend on previous market behavior and potential confirmation. Even though the long upper shadow suggests a failed rebound, there is some buying interest at the intraday level. Following a long downtrend, long black candlestick, or at help, attention shifts to proof of purchasing interest and a possible bullish upturn. The emphasis switches to the missed rally and a possible bearish turnaround after a lengthy uptrend, long white candlestick or opposition. Confirmation of Bearish or Bullish is required for both situations.

Hammer and Hanging Man

The Hammer and Hanging Man look exactly the same, but, based on the preceding price action, have different implications. They have actual thin limbs, lengthy lower shadows and limited or non-existent upper shadows (black or white). As for most configurations of single and double candlesticks, the Hammer and Hanging Man need approval before practice.

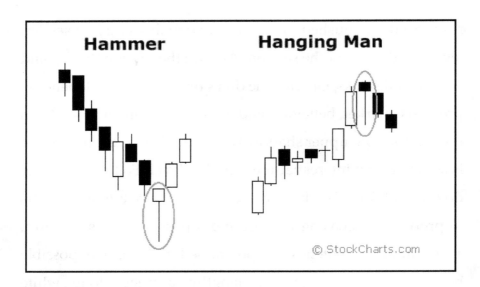

The Hammer is a bullish trend of turnaround, evolving after a fall. Besides a potential reversal of the pattern, hammers may even label bottoms or help rates. Hammers have indicated an optimistic resurgence following a fall. The long lower shadow's low suggests sellers pushed down rates throughout the session. The strong finish, though, indicates buyers have regained their footing to end the session on a strong note. Although this may seem appropriate to operate on, the hammers need more bullish proof. The hammer's low indicates there are still plenty of sales remaining. Further purchasing pressure is required before operating, and ideally on an increasing scale. Such confirmation may come from a white candlestick up the gap or large. Hammers are close to sale climaxes, and high volume may help to improve reversal validity.

The Hanging Man is a bearish pattern of reversal, which can also mark a level of top or resistance. A Hanging Man, forming after an advance, signals selling pressure is beginning to increase. The long lower shadow's low suggests sellers were driving down prices throughout the session. With the bulls regaining their feet and pushing up rates by the end, the emergence of sales pressure lifts the yellow flag. As with the Hammer, bearish affirmation is expected by a Hanging Man before the intervention. This clarification will arrive on a heavy volume like a gap down or long black candlestick.

Inverted Hammer and Shooting Star

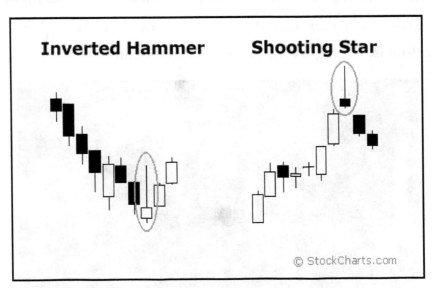

The Inverted Hammer and Shooting Star appear almost the same but, depending on past pricing activity, have distinct consequences. All candlesticks include actual thin bodies (black or white), large upper shadows, and lower shadows, which are tiny or absent. These candlesticks mark potential reversals of the pattern but require proof before practice.

Depiction of Bulls Vs. Bears

A candlestick is a reflection of the fight between Bulls (buyers) and Bears (sellers) over a given time. The comparison can be created between two football teams of this fight, which we may often name the Bulls and the Bears. The candlestick's bottom (intra-session low) reflects a touchdown for the Bears and a touchdown for the Bulls' peak (intra-session high). The higher the rise, the higher the Bulls are to a touchdown. The higher the bottom is, the higher the Bears are to a touchdown.

(Candlesticks showing up and down movement in the S&P 500 index)

Western Bar Charts

One of the fundamental methods of technical analysis is the bar map, where the open, near, strong, and low values of stocks or other financial securities are displayed in bars that are illustrated as a sequence of values over a specified period of time. To differentiate such charts from more conventional bar charts used to represent other forms of data, bar charts are also referred to as OHLC charts (open-high-low-close charts). Bar charts make it easier for the traders to see patterns. In other terms, each bar is, in reality, just a collection of 4 prices for a certain day, or any other time span, that is linked in a certain way by a bar — hence it is sometimes referred to as a price bar.

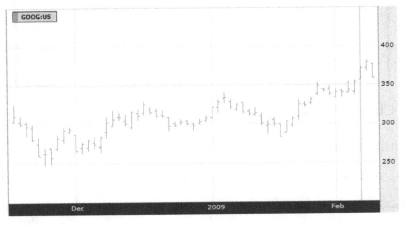

A price bar displays the opening price of the financial instrument as a left horizontal line, which is the price at the beginning of the time cycle, and the closing price as a right horizontal line, which is the last price for the duration. Such horizontal lines are classified as tick marks too. The top of the bar reflects the maximum quality, while the bottom of the bar portrays the low price. Unless the pricing bar is a constant price bar for a product, then the opening and closing rates are the sale values at the market opening and at the market closing, respectively. The high price is also the peak demand exchanged during the day, while the low price is the lowest price during the day.

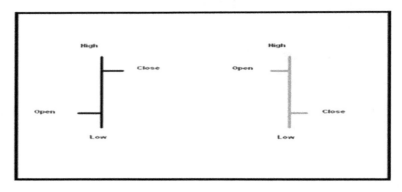

Bar Chart Patterns

Examination of the bar charts becomes more valuable as the bars are presented over a span of time, enabling the discernment of trends that can predict potential values with different degrees of effectiveness. The easiest analogy is between 2 consecutive bars. An up-day is when the closure is higher than the prior day. When the near is smaller, a down-day is. The closing price is usually regarded to be the most critical amount, as traders responded for the day to the news. But often the close is down, not because of poor reports, but because often traders sell overnight due to bad reports on close to prevent any market declines.

Higher closures usually suggest a bullish market feeling while lower closings show a bearish market feeling. An uptrend is a sequence of changes in which the peaks are mostly higher than the day before, and the lows are higher too. The uptrend is supported by both the lows higher and the closes higher (up-day). A downtrend is a reverse cycle, where peaks, drops, and closings on consecutive down-days are typically smaller.

Line Charts

The most common and easiest form of stock charts used in technical analysis is a line map. The line chart is often called a close-only map as it charts the underlying security's closing price, with a line connecting the dots created by the close point. On a line map, the market data for the underlying protection is plotted along the horizontal axis on a graph with the period plotted from left to right, or the x-axis and demand values plotted from the bottom up to the vertical axis, or the y-axis.

Inline charts, the price data used is typically the near price of the underlying security. The line chart's uncluttered simplicity is its greatest asset as it offers a simple, clearly identifiable, graphic representation of the price shift. This makes it an ideal tool for identifying the prevailing levels of support and resistance, trend lines, and certain patterns in the chart.

The line chart does not, however, indicate the highs and lows, and thus do not indicate the session price range. Despite this, line charts were Charles Dow's favorite charting technique, which was only interested in the level at which the price was closed. This, Dow thought, is the session or trading period's most valuable price details, as it calculated the unrealized benefit or loss of that time.

Numerous traders who believe that the closing price is the most relevant data and are not concerned with the uncertainty generated by market fluctuations and small price changes, or the volatility that characterizes the start of the trading day, tend to prefer line charts or close-only charts.

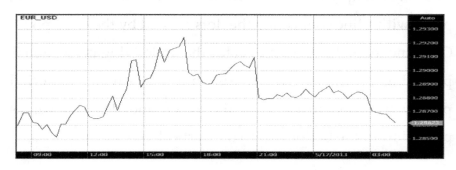

The above is a chart of the EUR/USD with a 15-minute **time frame**.

5.6 Application of Technical analysis for trading Options and its Benefits

In short term trading, technical indicators are also used to enable the investor to recognize the trend and its trajectory.

Since options are prone to time decay, the retention period takes on value. A stock trader is allowed to retain a position forever, while an options trader is constrained by the fixed time specified by the expiry date of the options. Due to time constraints, momentum indicators are common among options traders, which appear to identify levels of overbought and oversold.

Relative Strength Index – RSI

For options on specific securities, RSI fits well. The strongest candidates for short-term trading dependent on RSI are the options for extremely liquid, high-beta stocks.

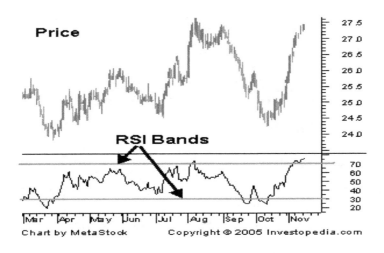

Chart by MetaStock   Copyright © 2005 Investopedia.com

Bollinger Bands

The value of volatility is known to all options traders, and Bollinger bands are a common way to calculate volatility. When volatility rises, the bands extend and contract when volatility declines. The more the price travels to the upper band, the more the security can be overbought, and the more the price rises to the lower band, the more it may be oversold.

A shift of prices beyond the bands will indicate that the security is ripe for a turnaround, and traders of options should position themselves appropriately.

Intraday Momentum Index – IMI

For high-frequency option traders seeking to gamble on intraday movements, the Intraday Momentum Index is a strong technical indicator. It incorporates the principles of intraday candlesticks and RSI, thereby offering an acceptable range for intraday trading (similar to RSI) by suggesting degrees of overbought and oversold. Utilizing IMI, an options trader could be able to spot possible opportunities at an intraday correction to execute a bullish trade in an up-trending market or to execute a bearish trade at an intraday price bump in a down-trending market.

Money Flow Index – MFI

A momentum indicator that incorporates price and volume data is the Money Flow Index. It is often referred to as RSI volume-weighted. The MFI metric calculates the cash inflow and outflows into an asset over a specified period of time.

MFI is best adapted for stock-based options trading (as opposed to index-based) and longer-duration trades due to reliance on volume data. This may be a leading sign of a trend transition as the MFI moves in the same direction as the stock price.

Put-Call Ratio (PCR) Indicator

Using put options against call options, the put-call ratio calculates trading volume. The shifts in its value, regardless of the actual put-call ratio's value, signify a shift in general market sentiment.

The ratio is above 1 when there are more puts than calls, suggesting bearishness. The ratio is less than 1, suggesting bullishness, while call volume is greater than put volume. The put-call ratio, however, is often regarded by traders as a contrary measure.

Open Interest – OI

Open interest shows possibilities for open or unsettled contracts. OI does not generally imply a particular uptrend or downtrend, but it does include indicators of a given trend's intensity. Rising open interest implies fresh capital inflow and, thus, the longevity of the current trend, while a slowing pattern implies a declining OI.

5.7 Mindset and Trading Psychology

Trading of securities is about profit, stop-loss and benefit. On the opposite, trading in options is about a time frame and potential opportunities. Your emphasis is at the initial price at which you execute your order and your profit and loss. You concentrate on static points and an unknown point in time for the opportunity or loss to be created by the trade.

From the outset, options trades are built to recognize how the outcome looks and how long you have to wait to make that outcome happen. Many trade options provide a window of opportunity during which they can earn money in a trade and gain a return in several situations. You make a directional decision in stock markets. Only one scenario creates a return.

The trading of options depends on keeping and changing before the end. Under a "price tent," keep and adjust over a given defined time frame. The emphasis is on the end target, and changes are anticipated and scheduled. In a price range, you work the trade and, if appropriate, change the window before the trade period has elapsed.

Trading psychology explained

One of the most important factors of being a successful trader is having the right mindset. Trading psychology relates to the mentality of an investor during his time in the markets. It will assess the degree to which they are effective in securing a profit, or it may offer an indication of why heavy losses have been suffered by a trader.

The primary goal of studying about trading psychology is to become conscious of the different dangers identified with a significant negative trait and to establish more optimistic qualities. Traders well-versed in the dynamics of investing would normally not operate on prejudice or sentiment. Therefore, they are more likely to produce a return throughout their tenure on the exchanges or to mitigate their losses.

Improve your trading psychology

By being conscious of your own feelings, perceptions and personality characteristics, enhancing your trading psychology will most effectively be accomplished. When these have been identified, you should put in place a trading strategy that takes these variables into consideration in the hope of minimizing any effects they may have on your decision-making.

For example, rather than incurring a minor loss on your trading portfolio, you might let losses run with the expectation that the market would rebound. This might result in higher losses.

You may use stops to offset this to decrease your risks and to determine when to close a certain transaction before you open the trade. By doing so, when you have made a deliberate effort not to rely on them, but rather, you have taken action to counteract them, you have become mindful of your own prejudices and thoughts.

Biases are a personal inclination in favor of one item over another. This is because trading preference means that you will be more likely to trade an asset on which you have had prior performance or to avoid an asset on which a historical loss has occurred. It is necessary for traders to be mindful of their conscious prejudices.

Identify your personality traits

Recognizing your personality traits from the outset is one of the secrets to delivering successful trading psychology. If you have impulsive behavior or if you are inclined to behaving out of indignation or irritation, you would need to be realistic with yourself.

Develop and follow a trading plan

To ensure that you accomplish your targets, having a trading strategy is paramount. A trading plan serves as the template for your trading, and your time obligations, trading funds available, your risk-reward ratio, and a trading strategy you are secure with should be illustrated.

Be adaptive

While having a trading strategy is critical, note that no two days are the same on the markets. If there is more uncertainty on one day and the markets change, especially unpredictably, you can plan to place your trading operation on pause before you are confident that you know what is happening.

Bottom line

Trading psychology is more about your attitude, and it will inform an indication of your gains or losses. Before initiating a trade, it is necessary for you to be mindful of your own

shortcomings and prejudices, but it is also vital that you recognize your own strengths.

Conclusion

Trading in options is generally about getting an advantage against other traders, and you are instantly ahead by narrowly restricting your trades to companies and sectors that you recognize and have studied.

The majority of people claim it is dangerous to trade options and purchase calls/puts. Nevertheless, it is a mistaken idea that traders can easily mint money from options trading or go bankrupt. Uninformed individuals who claim this tend to pursue the assumption that when they expire out of the money, such that, below the calls' strike price and above the strike price of puts, 80% of options expire without profit. This is dead wrong; as prior to expiration, many options are executed.

This would rely a great deal on what your risk level is, how aged you are, what platform you use, and so on. Just 2-5 percent of your portfolio should be devoted to a single trade. There are examples of traders who bet on trades a couple hundred thousand dollars. It is strongly recommended to avoid making such a mistake. Even if you are completely fine about it, you must not ruin your investments.

Each option has a date of expiry — a date that is either worth value or meaningless to that option. An option has no worth when its call option's strike price is greater than the price of the underlying, and when the strike price is below the price of the underlying contract, it is worth something (in the money). At any moment, you can execute the options, but if they are in the money, they will be immediately exercised at their expiry.

Then arises the issue of when the options can be exercised. If you deal with huge capital, the chances are that you're just going to be trading premiums. If you have the funds to really exercise (buy 100 stock shares at the strike price), then if you exercise rather than indulge in option's trading, or are out of the money, and are optimistic on the market, you can gain more money, so go ahead and exercise anytime you like.

You should have a specified timetable when entering an options activity. If you have no idea when you intend to sell or what you intend to do if the underlying falls to x value, almost every time, definitely, you would utterly collapse and lose cash. Take the revenue you earn, take the gain if you earn 100 percent+ on a transaction.

Although there are loads of indicators correlated with options that traders stand by, you can rely on four key indicators.

Delta can assess the option's vulnerability to market fluctuations of the underlying stock. Usually, this would be defined as a number between 1 and -1, where 0 to 1 is for calls, and -1 to 0 is for puts. The scale demonstrates how high the price of the option will increase if the price of the underlying commodity is moved to $1.

Gamma is the rate of a shift in the variance of an option per 1-point shift in the value of the underlying stock. In order to retain a hedge over a larger price spectrum, a delta hedge approach aims to minimize gamma.

Mathematically, gamma is the first delta derivative that is used in an effort to calculate the market change of an option compared to the sum of money it is in or out of. In the same respect, with respect to the underlying interest, gamma is the second derivative of an option's price. Gamma is minimal when the option being determined is deep in or out of the money. When the option is close or at the money, gamma is at its best. For minor adjustments in the price of the underlying stock, Gamma measurements are the most reliable. The long-position options include a positive gamma, whereas a negative gamma is valid for all short options.

Theta is a calculation of an option's time decay, the dollar sum an option would eliminate due to the passing of time every day. Theta grows when an option hits the end date for in the money options. Theta falls when an option reaches expiration for in the money and out of the money options.

Theta is one of the essential terms to be grasped by a beginning options investor since it describes the influence of time on the price of the bought or sold options. Buying longer-term contracts are preferable if you choose to buy an option. You'll like to short the shorter-term options if you want a plan that benefits from time decay because the reduction of value attributable to time occurs fast.

Before initiating an options trade, the first task is to understand what options are and how they will work with the overall trading plan. You may create trading ideas that fit with a particular approach for options with an understanding of how options operate. After a possible trade-in option has been identified, you can build a detailed strategy that includes developing an entry and exit plan. If you can discipline yourself to monitor and manage a trade after its initiation, you can definitely maximize your likelihood of a lucrative outcome.